George Villiers,

Second Duke of Buckingham

Twayne's English Authors Series

Bertram H. Davis, Editor
Florida State University

TEAS 394

GEORGE VILLIERS, SECOND DUKE OF BUCKINGHAM
(1628–1687)
Portrait from the Collection of The Earl of Jersey

George Villiers, Second Duke of Buckingham

By John H. O'Neill

Hamilton College

Twayne Publishers • *Boston*

George Villiers,
Second Duke of Buckingham

John H. O'Neill

Copyright © 1984 by G. K. Hall & Company
All Rights Reserved
Published by Twayne Publishers
A Division of G. K. Hall & Company
70 Lincoln Street
Boston, Massachusetts 02111

Book Production by Marne B. Sultz

Book Design by Barbara Anderson

Printed on permanent/durable acid-free
paper and bound in the United States of
America.

Library of Congress Cataloging in Publication Data

O'Neill, John H.
    George Villiers, Second Duke of Buckingham.

    (Twayne's English authors series; TEAS 394)
    Bibliography: p. 137
    Includes index.
    1. Buckingham, George Villiers, Duke of, 1628–1687—
Criticism and interpretation.   I. Title.   II. Series.
PR3328.B5O6   1984   822'.4   83-26529
ISBN 0-8057-6880-7

For my children,
John Markos O'Neill
and
Amy Elizabeth O'Neill

Contents

About the Author
Preface
Acknowledgments
Chronology

    Chapter One
    The Life of the Duke of Buckingham   1

    Chapter Two
    Buckingham's Nondramatic Poetry and Prose   21

    Chapter Three
    Buckingham's Minor Dramatic Works   52

    Chapter Four
    The Rehearsal   81

    Chapter Five
    Buckingham's Reputation and Influence   111

Notes and References   127
Selected Bibliography   137
Index   142

About the Author

John H. O'Neill was born in Madison, Wisconsin, and educated at Wisconsin State College, LaCrosse, and the University of Minnesota. Since 1972 he has been a member of the Department of English at Hamilton College, Clinton, New York, where he is now a professor. His articles and reviews have appeared in *Eighteenth-Century Studies, Clio, Tennessee Studies in Literature,* the *Durham University Journal, Restoration, Eighteenth-Century Life, Papers on Language and Literature,* and *Early American Literature.* Professor O'Neill is a member of the editorial board of *Restoration: Studies in English Literary Culture, 1660–1700.* He is now working on an edition of the court poetry of the Restoration.

Preface

Perhaps no group of writers in English literary history is so fascinatingly alien to us as the Restoration court wits. Their brilliant, extravagant lives, their sparkling conversational wit, their multiplicity of interests and talents, and above all their willingness to experiment with the forbidden in both thought and behavior—all these beckon to us across the centuries. On the other hand, their literary work, the product of a sensibility formed by conditions long since past, seems to us sometimes trivial and slight, sometimes maddeningly, unnecessarily complex.

The twentieth century has treated the earl of Rochester, Sir George Etherege, and many of their contemporaries, particularly George Villiers, second duke of Buckingham, with this combination of eager interest and puzzled unfamiliarity. Three times in the twentieth century Buckingham has been the subject of fascinated biographers. But critics have ignored nearly all his work except for his masterpiece, *The Rehearsal*, and even that has more often been studied for its influence on later writers than for itself. This book is the first critical study to treat the whole body of Buckingham's work as the product of a single mind.

The personal and literary character of the duke of Buckingham is reminiscent, at least to an American student of his work, of that of the nineteenth-century American humorist, Mark Twain. Both men were exciting speakers known for their extemporaneous wit—Twain on the lecture platform, Buckingham in the House of Lords. Like Twain, Buckingham was fascinated by technology and innovation, and like Twain, he lost a fortune investing in promising schemes. Like Twain, Buckingham spent the last years of his life thinking and writing about religion, attacking what he felt was the hypocrisy and narrow-mindedness of religious orthodoxy. Most important, Buckingham, like Mark Twain, was both attracted and repelled by social and literary propriety and gentility. Both men longed for respectability, both wrote their least successful work when they sought it, and both achieved their greatest successes when they satirized it.

Buckingham's most successful works incorporate a fruitful creative tension between the orthodoxies of his time and the impulse to de-

GEORGE VILLIERS, SECOND DUKE OF BUCKINGHAM

part from them or to mock them. His elegy for General Fairfax challenges conventional ideas of political and military greatness, redefining greatness as the ability to choose a virtuous simplicity in private and public conduct. The style of the poem, plain and sometimes even homely, is apparently at odds with its Pindaric form. In *The Chances*, the heroic virtue of Don Frederick and the First Constantia are contrasted with the frank language and realistic sexuality of Don John and the Second Constantia. In *The Rehearsal* the contrast is between the wild imagination of Bayes, which outrages dramatic propriety, and the sober and detached judgment of Smith and Johnson, which upholds that propriety. And in his epigrams, Buckingham was often able to juxtapose opposites in a way which acutely heightens the contrasts.

On the other hand, Buckingham's artistic failures usually arise from an inability to maintain that creative tension—a tendency to exaggerate the contrasts, or to make one quality too weak to remain in balance with its opposite. For example, the poem "To His Mistress" contrasts the appeal of the body to that of the mind, but the expressions are too conventional to make the tension believable or interesting. In *The Battle of Sedgmoor Rehearsed at Whitehall*, the contrast between the stupidity of Feversham and the ironic detachment of the lord and lady who interrogate him is overdrawn. In *The Restauration*, Buckingham's effort to "purify" both the characters and the action—to separate the comic from the tragic, the base from the noble—deprives the play of the complexity which might make its characters human. Thus the complexity of Buckingham's personal character was an artistic principle as well. Insofar as he could create this complexity in his work, he succeeded; when, in compliance with his understanding of the critical doctrines of his time, he tried to simplify, he failed.

No collected edition of Buckingham's works has been published since the eighteenth century, and none is readily available today. Two plays, *The Rehearsal* and *The Country Gentleman*, have recently been published in scholarly editions; both are excellent, and I have used them. For Buckingham's other works I have been forced to use rarer editions. I have used the first editions of his play *The Chances* and his prose tract, *A Short Discourse*. For his published poems I have used the one-volume edition published in Glasgow by Robert Urie in 1752, simply because a copy of that edition was available in the Burke Library at Hamilton College. On the poems quoted in this study it differs from the first editions of Buckingham's *Miscellaneous*

Preface

Works (2 vols., 1704–5) only in capitalization and punctuation. For the remaining plays and prose works I have used the edition of Buckingham's works prepared but never published by Bishop Thomas Percy in the late eighteenth century. This edition is the most authoritative collected one for all Buckingham's works, but since only a very few copies exist, I have used it only when there was no alternative.

John H. O'Neill

Hamilton College

Acknowledgments

I wish to acknowledge obligations to the Publications Board of the University of Durham for permission to quote from Buckingham's *The Rehearsal*, edited by D. E. L. Crane; to Yale University Press for permission to quote from the *Poems on Affairs of State*, edited by George deForest Lord; to the Clarendon Press for permission to quote from *The Poems and Letters of Andrew Marvell*, edited by H. M. Margoliouth; to the University of Pennsylvania Press for permission to quote from Buckingham's and Sir Robert Howard's *The Country Gentleman*, edited by Arthur H. Scouten and Robert D. Hume; to the Cambridge University Press for permission to quote from *The Dramatic Works in the Beaumont and Fletcher Canon*, edited by Fredson Bowers; to the University of California Press for permission to quote from *The Works of John Dryden*, edited by H. T. Swedenberg, Jr., Earl Miner, Vinton A. Dearing, and George R. Guffey; and *The Diary of Samuel Pepys*, edited by Robert Latham and William Matthews; to Harcourt Brace Jovanovich, Inc., for permission to quote from *Eighteenth-Century English Literature*, edited by Geoffrey Tillotson, Paul Fussell, Jr., and Marshall Waingrow; and to the earl of Jersey for permission to quote from the duke of Buckingham's commonplace book and to reproduce the portrait which appears as the frontispiece of this book.

I am extremely grateful to the trustees of Hamilton College for a faculty fellowship which provided me the time to write a large portion of this study.

I also wish to acknowledge with the deepest gratitude the assistance of many friends and colleagues without which I could neither have begun nor finished this work. The late Professor Samuel Holt Monk of the University of Minnesota first helped me to understand the symmetrical complexity of Restoration and eighteenth-century literature. Professor David M. Vieth of Southern Illinois University and Professor Emeritus John Harold Wilson of Ohio State University have given me much advice and encouragement and have shared with me the knowledge accumulated in many years of pioneering study of the Restoration court wits. Professor Cameron C. Nickels of James Madison University and my mother, Jean H. O'Neill, have both read large

GEORGE VILLIERS, SECOND DUKE OF BUCKINGHAM

sections of this manuscript and have offered advice which I have gratefully accepted. Professor Frederick Wagner, chairman of the department of English at Hamilton College, has patiently read the entire manuscript, parts of it several times. I flatter myself that the ideas which his suggestions helped me to recognize and express were present, if latent, in my own mind. Finally, to my wife, Mary O'Neill, whose love has enriched my life and work since I have first known her and with whom I have always shared whatever ideas most excited me, I owe more gratitude than I can express.

Chronology

- 1628   George Villiers born 30 January to George Villiers, first duke of Buckingham, and Katherine, duchess of Buckingham. 23 August, his father assassinated.
- ca. 1641   Enters Trinity College, Cambridge, where he forms friendship with Abraham Cowley.
- 1642   Awarded Master of Arts degree. Leaves Cambridge to join king's army in Civil War. Sent to the Continent.
- 1648   Returns to England to join royalist forces. Buckingham esstates confiscated by Parliament.
- 1650   Accompanies King Charles II to Scotland to form alliance against Lord Protector Cromwell.
- 1651   July, takes part in Charles's unsuccessful invasion of England.
- 1657   7 September, marries Mary Fairfax, daughter of Thomas, third Lord Fairfax, general for Parliamentary forces. Imprisoned by Cromwell in Tower of London.
- 1660   English monarchy restored. Buckingham takes active role in the Restoration.
- 1663   Thwarts attempt by Abraham Goodman, a servant, to assassinate him.
- 1665   Naval war breaks out between England and Holland. Buckingham attempts unsuccessfully to obtain a command.
- 1666   Begins intrigue with Anna-Maria, countess of Shrewsbury.
- 1667   Completes and presents adaptation of *The Chances*, originally written by John Fletcher; February, play performed on stage. Defeats plot by his enemies to convict him of treason and engineers fall from power of earl of Clarendon, chief of his enemies. Joins "Cabal" ministry.
- 1668   January, fights fatal duel with earl of Shrewsbury. In House of Lords, introduces bill to relax laws against religious nonconformists, but bill fails to pass.
- 1669   *The Country Gentleman*, written jointly by Buckingham

GEORGE VILLIERS, SECOND DUKE OF BUCKINGHAM

and Sir Robert Howard, ridicules Sir William Coventry and leads to his fall from power.

1670 Negotiates public treaty of Dover with France, unaware of terms of secret treaty.

1671 January, illegitimate son born to Buckingham and countess of Shrewsbury but dies soon thereafter. May, Buckingham elected chancellor of Cambridge University. December, *The Rehearsal*, Buckingham's most successful play, produced.

1672 Writes *Letter to Sir Thomas Osborn* in justification of war with Holland.

1674 Impeached by the House of Commons, dismissed from all posts by King Charles, and fined by House of Lords for cohabitation with countess of Shrewsbury. After brief retirement from public affairs, joins parliamentary opposition.

1675 Speaks in House of Lords against new Test Act; introduces Bill of Indulgence to protect religious freedom. Both efforts unsuccessful.

1677 Confined in Tower of London for arguing that Parliament, prorogued for more than a year, is dissolved; June, released.

1680 Exclusion crisis. Buckingham becomes popular figure in opposition party.

1681 Opposition party falls from popular favor. Buckingham attacked by Dryden as "Zimri" in *Absalom and Achitophel*.

1683 Completes revision of Beaumont's and Fletcher's *Philaster* as *The Restauration*; play not performed.

1685 *A Short Discourse upon the Reasonableness of Men's Having a Religion, or Worship of God.*

1686 Retires to Castle Helmsley, Yorkshire, to hunt, read, and write.

1687 Buckingham dies in farmhouse at Kirkby Moorside, Yorkshire, 16 April.

Chapter One
The Life of the Duke of Buckingham

Birth and Family Background

Perhaps no English author ever began life with more advantages of wealth and position than George Villiers. His father was the first duke of Buckingham, who by means of the favor of King James I had risen from obscurity to become the most powerful man in the kingdom. Attracted by the elder Villiers's physical beauty and his bold and active manner, King James had made him first his cupbearer, then Master of the Horse, Lord High Admiral, and finally, in 1623, duke of Buckingham, the first English duke outside the royal family since 1572.

The rapidity of the first duke's rise and the ease with which he accomplished it won him many enemies, and the policies he pursued after he gained power made many more. He attempted in 1623 to arrange a marriage between Prince Charles, the heir apparent, and the daughter of the king of Spain. When the negotiations were broken off, he induced Parliament to declare war. Then, as commander of the English forces, he suffered a series of disastrous failures which culminated in his unsuccessful siege of the fortress of St. Martin's, in the Isle of Rhé, where within twenty days he lost four thousand men, more than half his army.

In common with his father, the younger George Villiers had a charming manner—Louis XIV once paid him the compliment of saying that he was "almost the only English *gentleman* he had seen"[1]—a ready wit, a mistrust of any authority higher than his own, a taste for political maneuvering, and an almost touchingly stubborn faith that by the sheer force of his will he could bring about governmental measures regardless of their inherent wisdom. Unlike his father, who was a connoisseur of the arts but had no creative talent, the second duke applied his wit to writing poetry, prose, and drama.

Young George was born on 30 January 1628 and christened on 14 February. The king—now Charles I, for James had died in 1625—stood as godfather, together with the earl of Suffolk; and the queen, Henrietta Maria, was godmother. Dr. Laud, the most powerful prelate in the Church of England, performed the baptism. Within a few years, all these principals except the queen were to die violently, and the world into which George Villiers was born was to change completely.

In August of the same year, the first duke of Buckingham was assassinated by Lieutenant John Felton, a half-mad naval officer who believed that in killing the duke he was freeing England from "the cause of all our miseries; the grievance of grievances," as the House of Commons had characterized him in its Petition of Right asking, ineffectually, for his impeachment. The assassination of his father was the first of a lifelong series of sudden changes of fortune for young Villiers. When his mother, who had begun life as a Roman Catholic and had joined the Church of England only as a necessary preliminary to her marriage, was reconverted to Catholicism, the young duke and his brother Francis—his father's posthumously born son—were taken into the royal family, where they were brought up and educated as companions to the two young princes of the blood royal, Charles and James.

Youth

At about the ages of twelve and eleven, respectively, George and Francis Villiers were sent to Cambridge University, from which George received the degree, largely ceremonial, of Master of Arts in 1642. At Cambridge Buckingham met Abraham Cowley, who was to become, after the publication of his collection of love poems, *The Mistress* (1647), and of his epic, the *Davideis* (1656), one of the most prominent poets of his time. The friendship which began when the two men were schoolmates continued until the poet's death in 1667, when Buckingham paid for an elegant and expensive funeral. In 1663, Buckingham purchased a farm in Chertsey and gave it to Cowley as a place in which to spend his last years in retirement. Despite the differences in their fortunes and dispositions, it seems likely that the two men developed their tastes for wit together. But Cowley, influenced by the Donne tradition, typically exercised the kind of wit that astonishes the reader by its perception or discovery of "occult resemblances in things apparently unlike,"[2] whereas Buckingham, writing and speaking as a "man of wit" at the height of the Restoration, exercised a kind of wit which provokes mirth through its discovery of incongruous differences between things apparently similar. Cowley often aspired to show his learning; Buckingham was impelled both by his temperament and by the manners of a nobleman to wear his very lightly.

Another schoolfellow was Martin Clifford, a young man with a satirical wit more like Buckingham's own, whom the duke in later years was to make his secretary and occasional collaborator in literary compositions, including *The Rehearsal*.

In late 1642, the English Civil War, with the Parliamentary forces on one side and the Royalists on the other, broke out. The young Villiers brothers—George was now fifteen and Francis fourteen—slipped away from Cambridge to join King Charles's army at Oxford. When the Royalist forces under Prince Rupert and Lord Gerard stormed Lichfield Close on 10 April 1643, both brothers took an active part in the battle. The reaction to their first military experience was swift: Parliament sequestered their estates as punishment for their taking up arms against it, and their relatives and guardians arranged that they be sent to the Continent, where they might continue their education without the interruptions and dangers of war.

On the Continent the two young men stayed primarily in Florence and Rome. They did not enroll in a university, but traveled under the direction of a tutor, as was the custom for young Englishmen of means and position, on what was called the Grand Tour. One of the objectives of the Grand Tour was to enable a young man to acquire a familiarity with the modern foreign languages (he would have studied the ancient ones at school since boyhood) and the kind of social polish attainable only in the great continental courts. That Buckingham succeeded in his search for polish is attested by many of his contemporaries, including quite hostile judges. Dean Francis Lockier said, "That Duke of Buckingham was reckoned the most accomplished man of the age, in riding, dancing, and fencing. When he came into the presence chamber, it was impossible for you not to follow him with your eye as he went along, he moved so gracefully."[3] The French Comte de Grammont wrote, "He knew how to act all parts, with so much grace and pleasantry, that it was difficult to do without him, when he had a mind to make himself agreeable."

Bishop Burnet wrote, "He was a man of noble appearance and of a most lovely wit, wholly turned to mirth and pleasure."[4] And Edward Hyde, earl of Clarendon, who was thrown from power by Buckingham's influence, wrote in his memoirs, "His quality and condescension, the pleasantness of his humour and conversation, the extravagance and sharpness of his wit, unrestrained by any modesty or religion, drew persons of all affections and inclinations to like his company."[5] In May 1646, George and Francis were in Paris on their way home to London; they renewed their acquaintance with Prince Charles at the French court. They were back in London in the spring of 1647.

Charles I was now a prisoner of the Parliamentary forces (he was to be tried by Parliament in 1648 and executed in January 1649), and fighting had nearly ceased. In the summer of 1648, George and Francis Villiers plotted with Henry Rich, earl of Holland, to lead an uprising on the king's behalf. The uprising was unsuccessful. In a battle near Surbiton Common, the nineteen-year-old Francis Villiers was surrounded by a company of Parliamentary soldiers who attempted to take him prisoner. When he refused their demand for his surrender, he was killed. George escaped from the battlefield and fled to France.

The years that followed were full of plots—plots to return to England and "compound" with the Parliament for the return of his confiscated estates, plots to spy for the Royalists, and plots to bring the new king, Charles II, to the throne. In 1650 Buckingham accompanied the exiled king to Scotland to treat with the Covenanters and to prepare another military expedition. This was Charles's invasion of England from the north, launched in the late summer of 1651, and decisively defeated at the Battle of Worcester. Buckingham was again distinguished for his courage in battle, but he aroused the king's displeasure by requesting to be made commander in chief of the invading force and by sulking when he was refused in consequence of his youth.

The pride which occasioned this breach between King Charles and the duke was one of Buckingham's most obtrusive and troublesome characteristics throughout his life. Having been raised as Charles's companion, he felt himself equal to the king in social position, and perhaps his intellectual superior. Years later, during the Exclusion Crisis of 1679–80, he even told the French ambassador, Barillon, that he felt he had a claim to the succession to the throne: "Some times, after he has supped, Buckingham lets drop that through his mother, who descended from Edward IV., he inherits the claims of the House of Plantagenet."[6]

The years of exile on the Continent were difficult for all the Royalists, and particularly for Buckingham. His continued loyalty to the king—carried to such a degree that he repeatedly risked his life, not only in military engagements but also as a spy, to work for the restoration of the monarchy—was not appreciated by Charles or his closest adviser, Lord Clarendon. Though the duke had been born to great riches, his property had been seized by Parliament and given to others (principally to the Parliamentary general, Lord Fairfax), and he was forced to sell his father's collection of paintings by Rubens, Titian, and other masters in order to pay his ordinary expenses. Though he was repeatedly invited to "compound" with the Parliament—that is, to pledge his loyalty to it and swear not to take up arms against it—he always refused to do so. But he was now twenty-eight years old. The money from the sale of his father's art collection was running out. It was necessary to make some decisive change in his condition.

In June of 1657, therefore, Buckingham returned to England and began to maneuver for a way to make his peace with the Protectorate. He attempted unsuccessfully to meet with Cromwell. The Lord Protector had Buckingham watched closely, but he made no move to restrict his freedom of movement. No doubt he was waiting to see what Buckingham would do. Soon Buckingham began to pay court to Mary Fairfax, the daughter of the general to whom his own estates had been given. Though Lord Thomas Fairfax and his wife were severe and conservative judges of character, and although they could have no mercenary motive, since they were already in possession of part of Buckingham's estates, they approved of the match. Mary, however, was already betrothed, to Philip Stanhope, third earl of Chesterfield, and the banns had twice been read, but that engagement was broken off as, under the influence of Buckingham's considerable charm, her affections turned to him. "All his trouble in wooing was, he came, saw, and conquered," wrote Mary's cousin Brian Fairfax.[7]

Buckingham's new father-in-law, Lord Thomas Fairfax, was one of the few persons for whom the duke retained a lifelong respect. United both by the marriage and by mutual esteem, the two men began working and planning for the restoration of the monarchy, which they were certain would follow Cromwell's death, and which they expected could not be achieved without some renewal of the civil war.

Cromwell, angered at an alliance between a Parliamentary general and a high-ranking Royalist, ordered Buckingham seized and confined to the Tower of London. Though Lord Fairfax went to London to plead with the Lord Protector for his release, Cromwell would not relent. The Fairfax family feared that Buckingham might even be executed. But just at that time, Cromwell himself died. Buckingham wrote later, "I confess I was not a little delighted with the noise of the great guns, for I presently knew what it meant, and if Oliver had lived for three days longer I had certainly been put to death."[8]

When the Restoration came a year later, it was bloodless. George Monck, the commander of the Parliamentary army in Scotland, brought his army into England to guarantee the election of a "free Parliament" which could end military rule and recall the king. He enlisted the aid of Lord Fairfax, who raised a Yorkshire militia and joined him. Buckingham, now released from the Tower, accompanied his father-in-law, but because ex-Parliamentary officers would not serve under a well-known Royalist, he had to accept a staff position rather than a command. After the king's landing at Dover, Buckingham arranged to ride to London with him and share his triumph. The duke was now thirty years old.

Maturity

After the Restoration, Buckingham was himself restored. The estates which had been sequestered or confiscated were returned to him. His income, which at twenty thousand pounds a year was reputed the greatest in England, began again. Free to indulge himself, he developed numerous interests. He formed a circle of fashionable intellectuals—Abraham Cowley, Martin Clifford, Thomas Sprat, Edmund Waller, Sir John Denham, Christopher Wren, Sir Charles Sedley, Charles Sackville, and several others—who discussed literature and natural science. He assembled a stable of horses to race at Newmarket and to ride to hounds. He established a complete chemical laboratory at Wallingford House, staffed by a professional chemist, where he could conduct experiments. He became a member of the Royal Society and participated in its experiments and discussions. He maintained a string quartet of professional musicians, for whom he sometimes composed music, and he became a skilled violinist. He wrote poetry and plays. He pursued women, almost always successfully. He gave extravagant parties, at which both wit and wine flowed liberally, and at which

King Charles was often a guest. And in addition to all these pursuits, he plunged himself into the intrigue of court politics, a series of struggles for power in which the rewards were often trivial and fleeting, and the risks enormous.

Unlike his famous father, Buckingham was temperamentally ill-fitted for the role of a statesman. Whereas soberer men devoted their full attention for years to politics, Buckingham engaged in statecraft only intermittently, in the intervals afforded him by his other pursuits. Whereas other statesmen pursued coherent policies—the destruction of French power, for example, or the exclusion of a Catholic heir from the English throne—Buckingham moved first one way, then another. (One important exception is his consistent advocacy of religious toleration, a foresighted and generous policy in which he achieved neither success nor reward.) The motive which consistently prompted him, the bait which led him on, was simply glory. His relish for the honors he received was almost childish. Before the magnificence of Louis XIV, the glorious "Sun King" of France, he was incapable of detached judgment. And whereas for other politicians—for his father, for example—power was an opportunity to accumulate wealth, Buckingham spent his vast fortune in the service of the king and of his own notions of glory, reducing himself to the verge of poverty and leaving nothing for his heirs. His impulsiveness led him to accept formidable risks, and, even more disastrously, his pride led him to underestimate the abilities of his opponents, to imagine that the rules which applied to others were irrelevant to him, and to consider that the honors he sought, as well as those he received, were no more than his due.

Buckingham in power. At the beginning of Buckingham's career as a statesman, the object of his intrigues was to destroy the power of the earl of Clarendon. Clarendon had been the king's advisor throughout his exile. His honesty and his devotion to the king are unquestionable to modern historians, and he may have known more about the art and policy of government than any other man of his time. But his ideas were growing out of date, and his sourly conservative morality annoyed King Charles. Buckingham's wit and gaiety were, by comparison, appealing, and whereas Clarendon lectured the king about his vices, Buckingham artfully encouraged them. He even assumed the role of a pimp when, in 1664, he conspired with lords Sandwich and Arlington to arrange an assignation between the king and Frances Stuart. The influence of the royal mistress on the king was profound, and many courtiers who aspired to influence promoted the interests of women whom they felt they could rely upon. But Buckingham's attempts to exercise influence in this way were unsuccessful, sometimes because, as with Louise de Querouale, the lady achieved her object but escaped the duke's control; sometimes because, as with Nell Gwynn, the lady became the king's mistress but had no head for intrigue; and sometimes because, as with Mistress Stuart, the lady balked at being used in that way.

Buckingham's intrigues against Clarendon, in addition to irritating the Lord Chancellor, made Buckingham another enemy who was in the long run more powerful. That enemy was Clarendon's son-in-law, James, duke of York. As the brother of King Charles, James was heir apparent to the throne unless Queen Catherine gave birth to an heir (she never did), and he did not share the king's love of Buckingham's playful and iconoclastic wit. In 1665, when England fought a naval war with the Dutch, King Charles made the duke of York the admiral of the fleet. Buckingham, though he had no experience in naval warfare, hastened to the duke's flagship to request a command, and, when he was refused, tried to appeal over the duke's head to the king. It was a foolish move, for the king refused to overrule his brother, and James never forgot Buckingham's attempt to outmaneuver him. But to Buckingham, York was a stupid man. Bishop Burnet reported, "The duke of Buckingham gave me once a short but severe character of the two brothers; it was the more severe, because it was true. The king could see things if he would, and the duke would see things if he could."[9]

In 1667, a plot against Buckingham, launched by his enemies, backfired and brought him the power he had sought. Buckingham's interest in astronomy had made him the acquaintance of a half-educated astronomer who called himself Dr. John Heydon. On the basis of fabricated and willfully misinterpreted evidence, Heydon was arrested and accused of plotting with Buckingham to cast the king's horoscope, a treasonable offense.[10] But because of Heydon's loyalty to the duke—he refused to confess falsely, even though he was tortured—and the activity of Buckingham's own agents, the plot collapsed. When Arlington and Clarendon, who had engineered the plot, insisted on a hearing in the king's presence, Buckingham carried off his defense magnificently. He demonstrated to the king that the letter asking for the horoscope, a key piece of evidence, had been written not by himself but by his sister, the duchess of Richmond, and that it contained no explicit mention of the king anyway. When the king agreed that

The Life of the Duke of Buckingham 9

the whole thing had been a mistake, the episode was over. Within a month Clarendon was in disgrace, dismissed from his posts, and had fled into exile in France, while the House of Lords, at Buckingham's instigation, called for his impeachment. For the next several years King Charles governed without a chief minister, and during much of that time Buckingham was the most powerful member of his Privy Council.

The duke's interest in writing for the stage developed soon after the Restoration and continued throughout his life. In 1667, his adaptation of *The Chances*, a comedy originally written by Fletcher in 1617, was brought to the London stage, where it had a successful run. Although his playwriting was one of many pursuits which distracted him from political activity, he sometimes made it serve his political purposes. In 1669, searching for an expedient to remove Sir William Coventry, another political enemy, from his post as a commissioner of the Treasury, Buckingham wrote a scene which ridiculed Coventry and inserted it in a play, *The Country Gentleman*, written by Sir Robert Howard, which was then being prepared for production. Coventry, hearing of the plot to mock him publicly, threatened a brutal reprisal (he said he "would have the impersonator's nose cut") and challenged Buckingham to a duel. In the Restoration dueling was socially accepted as the proper method of avenging injured honor among the gentry and the aristocracy, but officially it was illegal. Participation in a duel was punishable by imprisonment, and a duelist who killed his opponent could be charged with murder—although if he was a nobleman he usually received a pardon from the king. When Buckingham received Coventry's challenge, he made certain that the king heard of it before the duel could be fought, and Coventry was confined to the Tower of London and dismissed from his Treasury and Privy Council posts.

Buckingham's reluctance to cross swords with Coventry was not the result of cowardice. He had fought a duel in the previous year, one which had seriously damaged his reputation and was to have a profound effect on his career. The cause of the duel was his affair with Anna-Maria, countess of Shrewsbury, a beautiful, sensual, and dangerous woman. The affair apparently began in 1665 or early in 1666, and it soon became common knowledge in court circles. Restoration society held a double standard in sexual conduct. Among the upper classes, where marriages were commonly contracted as alliances between property-holding families, husbands were hardly expected to be faithful to their wives. Buckingham had previously amused himself with brief liaisons with maids of honor and encounters with women of lower rank, although his reputation for dalliance with women may have been overstated, even with his own connivance. (Samuel Pepys reported that when Buckingham met with his old crony, Major Wildman, and other political radicals, "he makes the King believe that he is with his wenches.")[11] But during the nine years that his relationship with the countess of Shrewsbury continued, he apparently was not involved with any other woman. The plain, pious, conventional duchess of Buckingham, whose devotion to her husband was evident throughout both their lives, made the best of the situation. She preserved a friendship with the countess and even accompanied her on a trip to France in 1670, when Lady Shrewsbury was pregnant with a child by Buckingham.

Lady Shrewsbury's husband, Charles Talbot, earl of Shrewsbury, ignored the affair for two years. He had no desire to provoke an open quarrel with Buckingham, who was not only the most powerful man in England but an accomplished swordsman as well. Eventually, however, the situation could not be ignored. In 1667 Lady Shrewsbury, sitting in the theater with the duke and duchess of Buckingham, was publicly insulted by one Harry Killigrew, who boasted himself a former lover of the countess. Buckingham chased Killigrew around the theater; Killigrew apologized, begged for his life, and the following day, fled into exile in France. The incident caused an uproar. Lady Shrewbury believed that she could clear her own name only by dropping out of society for a while, so she, too, retired to France, to a convent near Paris. And the earl of Shrewsbury, perhaps goaded by those of his relatives who were among Buckingham's political enemies, sent the duke a challenge to a duel.

At Shrewsbury's insistence, the duel was to be fought in the French style, where not only the principals but the seconds were expected to fight. Shrewsbury chose as his seconds two relatives, Sir John Talbot and Bernard Howard, both skilled swordsmen. Buckingham, who could perceive the extreme danger in the style of the duel and the character of his opponents, chose as his seconds Sir Robert Holmes, a naval officer, and Lieutenant William Jenkins, an officer of the Guards and ex-fencing master.

The duel was fought on 16 January 1688. The fighting was furious and without quarter. Lieutenant Jenkins, on the Buckingham side, was killed instantly on the field, and the duke ran Shrewsbury through the body, so that he was carried from the field unconscious. He died on 16 March, apparently from complications growing out of his wound. His right lung had been punctured by Buckingham's sword; the immediate cause of death may have been tuberculosis or pneumonia. The public was horrified. Though Buckingham could not have refused the challenge to the duel without being ridiculed for cowardice, he was now infamous as a man who had killed the husband of his mistress.

Public opinion was still more scandalized at what happened when the countess returned from her French convent a month later. Buckingham invited her to move into his own house, and his wife, the duchess, went home to stay with her father at Nun Appleton House. According to Pepys, "I am told also that the Countesse of Shrewsbery is brought home by the Duke of Buckingham to his house; where his Duchess saying that it was not for her and the other to live together in a house, he answered, 'Why, Madam, I did think so; and therefore have ordered your coach to be ready to carry you to your father's;' which was a devilish speech, but they say true; and my Lady Shrewsbry is there it seems."[12] Though the countess lived in Wallingford House no more than a few months, she and the duke made no effort to conceal their adultery during the six more years of their affair.

In February of 1671, Buckingham and Lady Shrewsbury became the parents of an illegitimate child, a son, whom they christened George Villiers, with the king standing as godfather. Buckingham's marriage to Mary Fairfax had produced no issue, and this birth seemed a proof of his virility and vigor. Delighted, he spoke of the child as the earl of Coventry (his own title at birth). But within a few days the child died. Buckingham was destined never to have another.

Since the fall of Clarendon, the administration of the English government had been conducted by a loose coalition of five ministers of the Privy Council, which was nicknamed, collectively, the Cabal. The name was a sort of acronym derived from the first initials of the five ministers—Clifford, Arlington, Buckingham, Ashley, and Lauderdale—but its resemblance to the Hebrew word *Kabala*, with its associations of secrecy and magic, gave it a fittingly sinister ring. Within the Cabal, and between its members and the other ministers of the Privy Council, there was a constantly shifting web of intrigues, as the ministers jostled each other to increase their power and influence. King Charles, whose reputation for laziness and indifference to public affairs concealed an acute intelligence and the ruthlessness of a chess master who recognizes the weakness of his position, used each of the ministers for his purposes. But he did not hesitate to sacrifice any of them to the plotting of his colleagues or the resentments of the Parliament, which could express its disapproval of the king's policies only by impeaching his ministers. Charles apparently genuinely liked Buckingham. In addition to the fact that they had grown up together, they both had plain, barren wives and exciting, termagant mistresses. Both men enjoyed scientific inquiry, the theater, and the pleasures of the bottle and the bedroom. They shared an aristocratic disdain for public opinion and conventional morality. But whereas Buckingham imagined that he could control Charles—he is reported to have said, "I do suffer him [to pursue foolish policies] that I may hereafter the better command him"[13]—Charles in fact used, outsmarted, deceived, and controlled Buckingham.

In 1669 Charles hatched a complicated scheme for an alliance between himself and King Louis XIV of France. At a secret meeting in St. James's Palace, he revealed to a select circle of intimates (including two members of the Cabal, Clifford and Arlington) that he had become a Roman Catholic. He proposed to ally himself with Louis in an effort to bring England back into the Catholic Church. To effect this plan, he enlisted the aid of his Catholic brother, the duke of York, and the other lords at the meeting.

In fact, Charles was both more intelligent and more cynical than any of those present. However sincere his conversion, he must have known that, after the religious and political troubles of the past sixty years, including his father's execution, there was no possibility of returning England to the faith that it had abandoned under Henry VIII and had resisted readopting under "Bloody" Mary Tudor a century earlier. Certainly it is true that he never allowed his new faith to be publicly revealed nor took any overt step toward Catholicizing his country. But he saw in the alliance with Louis a way of making himself independent of Parliament, and therefore capable of pursuing his own policies without check from any quarter.

In the secret Treaty of Dover, negotiated in 1670, Charles promised to declare war on Holland as an ally of France, to announce his conversion to Catholicism when a convenient time arose (it never did), and—in a provision which might have brought about his execution by Parliament if it had been discovered—to send for French troops to put down any rebellion by his subjects against the scheme to Catholicize them. In return, he was to receive secret subsidies from France amounting to about three hundred seventy-five thousand pounds sterling per year.[14]

Though Charles probably had no intention of carrying out the article of the treaty which referred to his conversion, he had to account publicly for the money he was to receive, and for that purpose he resolved to negotiate a second treaty, one which would contain the articles of the first without the conversion clause. Buckingham, who the members of the secret plot believed most likely to cause trouble, was selected to negotiate the public treaty—which he would be led to believe was the only treaty. Those who were privy to the real treaty— Charles himself, Louis XIV, the French ambassador, and the two Cabal members who were parties to the plot—all conspired to lead Buckingham on a merry chase. He was sent to France to negotiate a treaty. There he was royally entertained, and entirely deceived, by Louis. He was installed in a royal apartment at the palace of St. Germain, entertained at grand dinners and balls, and kept busy negotiating with those who knew what he did not, the terms of the real treaty. Finally, in December of 1670, the sham treaty was concluded and signed by both sides—the French ambassador for Louis XIV and all the members of the Cabal for England.

The year 1671 was an eventful one for Buckingham, a period during which his pride was first gratified and later offended, and during which he produced his best single dramatic work. His illegitimate son was born and died in February. In May, he was elected chancellor of Cambridge University, an honor for which he had contended with Lord Arlington, his chief rival in the Cabal. The ceremony of his installation on 7 June was an occasion for splendid pomp, something that Buckingham thrived upon. It took place not in Cambridge, but in London, where Buckingham had rented York House for the day. (It belonged to him but had been leased to the French ambassador because Buckingham could not afford to maintain it.) There was an academic procession through the streets of London to York House, where there were speeches and a banquet. Buckingham provided a feast for all assembled and sent the university three hundred pounds for the purchase of plate.

Intrigues by Arlington and other enemies of Buckingham resulted in a severe blow to the duke's pride and prestige later in the year. A provision of the 1670 Treaty of London had called for an army of 6,000 English soldiers to be under Buckingham's command in King

Louis XIV's campaign against Holland. Now Arlington, aided by a faction of other plotters, persuaded King Charles that such an army would be too expensive and that Buckingham would be an unreliable commander. Charles decided in October 1671, to reduce the force to 2,400 men and to assign the command to his illegitimate son, the duke of Monmouth, and to Arlington's brother-in-law, the earl of Ossory. Buckingham's outraged reaction made the king uncomfortable but did the duke's cause no good.

Finally, in December of the same year Buckingham's most successful play, *The Rehearsal*, was produced. The play was a collection of parodies of a large number of plays familiar to the theatergoing public of the Restoration, an era when actors, playwrights, and playgoers assumed each other's roles and knew each other well. In the character of Poet Bayes, the leading character of the farce, Buckingham poked fun in passing not only at the literary community, but also at his political enemies. Primary among these was the earl of Arlington, whose outmaneuvering of Buckingham had just dealt so severe a blow to his pride. Since Arlington had a black patch across his nose,[15] Buckingham had Bayes wear one. And the ridiculous events of the play not only parody the complications of the heroic drama but also allude farcically to the political affairs of the country. Many of the characters in the inner drama of the play are kings, princes, and intriguing politicians, and although there are no clearly topical allusions, certainly audiences must have laughed loudly in recognition when a foolish dialogue on the inner stage was interrupted by the following commentary:

> *Smith*: This is a very wise Scene, Mr. *Bayes*.
> *Bayes*: Ay, you have it right: they are both Politicians. (2. 4. 23–24)

The play was a great success, but however well it may have mocked the intrigues of state, those intrigues continued as before.

In the winter of 1672, the Cabal ministry took two actions which were eventually to cause its downfall. One was the Stop of the Exchequer. This was a scheme, originally proposed by Sir Thomas Clifford but assented to by the rest, whereby payments from the royal treasury (the Exchequer) to bankers who had lent money to the government were to be stopped for one year. The money thus saved was to be used, in place of tax funds voted by Parliament—because Parliament refused to vote the funds—to outfit the fleet for war. This default brought on a financial panic. Those who had deposited their money with the bankers simply lost it for a year, and several bankers failed. Confidence in the government's good faith took years to recover.

The second of the two actions was a declaration of war on Holland, which had been required by the Treaty of Dover. In the seventeenth century, England and Holland were rivals in trade. They fought three wars, in 1651–54, 1665–67, and 1672, as they contested for control of the seas. Buckingham argued in his *Letter to Sir Thomas Osborn* (1672) that such control was necessary to the prosperity—even to the survival—of England, and it is true that after England gained control she became, in the eighteenth and nineteenth centuries, the world's foremost maritime power and trading nation. Thus the war with Holland was compatible with the perceived interests of England. But it was unpopular with the public, at least after an initial burst of enthusiasm. However much most Englishmen wished to defeat the Dutch, they were highly suspicious of the power of the French king, a Roman Catholic widely suspected of aspiring to "universal monarchy." An alliance with King Louis seemed a greater threat to England than the Dutch navy and merchant fleet.

The war dragged on until 1674 with inconclusive results, in the face of increasing opposition from the Parliament and the public. Envoys were exchanged among the warring nations. In June of 1672 Buckingham and Arlington traveled to both Holland and France for negotiations, but no change in the status of the war was agreed on. The Dutch fought on against the French invaders on land and the English at sea. The members of the Cabal continued to intrigue against one another. When the Test Act, forbidding Roman Catholics to hold any public office, was passed in 1673, Lord Clifford was forced to resign his post as Lord Treasurer. Then Shaftesbury, who had aligned himself with the opposition to the war, was dismissed. Buckingham made overtures to the opposition himself, but by this time he was suspected of opportunism and was distrusted in all quarters. A gathering group of his enemies plotted his downfall.

When the Parliament opened in January of 1674, the paternal relatives of the young earl of Shrewsbury (the son of Buckingham's mistress; he was then thirteen years old) presented a petition to the House of Lords. They charged that the duke of Buckingham and the countess of Shrewsbury lived in open, unconcealed adultery, and they asked that the House require the two to behave decently. Adultery was not a criminal offense, but it was a breach of morality, and to have his private morals discussed openly on the floor of the House of Lords was a personal disgrace for Buckingham. He could not allow the charges to be made without speaking in response to them. Partly defending himself and partly admitting the charges, the duke asked the forgiveness of his peers and promised to behave better in the future. After the petition and Buckingham's response were debated at several meetings, the Lords ordered him not to "converse nor cohabit with the said Anna-Maria, countess of Shrewsbury, for the future," and required both the duke and the countess to put up bonds of ten thousand pounds each, an enormous sum, as security of their future good behavior.

The episode made an irreparable stain on Buckingham's personal reputation. He had in fact lived in open adultery with Lady Shrewsbury. He had acted in this affair, as in so many things, as if he were not bound by the laws that ruled other men. Now he was forced by an assembly of his peers to acknowledge his error.

At the same time there was a movement in the House of Commons to impeach Buckingham. Throughout January of 1674 he was forced to fight his Parliamentary war on two fronts, speaking in the Commons in answer to charges that he had mismanaged the king's foreign policy by the alliance with France and the war with Holland, and at the same time defending himself in the Lords against the charges of adultery. Eventually he lost both fights. Shortly after the Lords reached their verdict, the Commons voted to request that the king dismiss the duke of Buckingham from all his employments. The king, tired of his own disagreements with Buckingham and delighted to use him as a scapegoat for the failure of the royal policies, complied. Thus by the end of January 1674, Buckingham's political career was ruined, he was in a notorious social disgrace, and his fortune, spent over the years in pursuit of greatness, was gone.

Buckingham in opposition. For a year the once-great duke lived in retirement in Yorkshire, husbanding the small income he received from the sale of his posts in the royal household. But in the spring of 1675 he returned to London and began an alliance with the Country party, as the opposition, soon to be known as the Whigs, was then called. He continued to speak in Parliament in support of his favorite cause, a Bill of Indulgence for dissenting Protestants (that is, for a measure of freedom of religion for Protestants outside the

Church of England), but without success. Together with Shaftesbury he became titular chief of the parliamentary opposition.

Opposition was congenial to Buckingham's personality. No longer forced to bear responsibility for the actions of others, free to champion his favorite causes and to attack policies with which he disagreed, he threw his energies again into politics. Thomas Osborne, earl of Danby, a former protégé of Buckingham's, was now Lord Treasurer and chief of the administration, and as Buckingham began to be seen as an advocate of the rights of the people against the crown, he and Danby became bitter opponents. In February 1677, Danby induced the House of Lords to order Buckingham and three other opposition leaders to be imprisoned in the Tower of London, where they remained until June. But this persecution increased their popularity with the people. Buckingham found himself at last a hero, cheered by crowds as he drove through the streets of London.

In 1678 England was swept by rumors of a Popish Plot—that is, of a plot by Roman Catholics to murder King Charles and to place his brother James—whose Catholicism was now well known—on the throne. A London magistrate named Sir Edmund Berry Godfrey, who had been hearing testimony relating to the alleged plot, was found murdered on the morning of 17 October; the identity of his murderers has never been discovered. Convinced that the Catholics were about to strike, the Parliament set up an investigating committee with Buckingham and Shaftesbury at its head. There followed a small Reign of Terror in which some Catholics, convicted by perjured testimony and a frightened court, lost their lives, and the ministry of the earl of Danby fell from office.

Quite possibly, Buckingham, Shaftesbury, and the other Whig leaders may have known that there was no serious danger to the life of the king. Their real motive was to persuade the king to disavow the succession to his Catholic brother and arrange for a Protestant successor. One such successor might have been Charles's eldest illegitimate son, James Scott, duke of Monmouth. But in order to legitimize Monmouth the king would have had to declare that he had been married to Lucy Walters, Monmouth's mother, and that was a lie to which Charles would not consent. Nor would he, as Buckingham had repeatedly urged him to do when they were on good terms, divorce the queen on grounds of infertility and take another wife.

By 1681 the terror, now known as the Exclusion Crisis, ended, and the former inquisitors became the prey. Shaftesbury was tried for high treason, and although he was acquitted, he left England in disgrace. He died in 1683 in Holland. Buckingham was not harmed by official power, but neither did he retain any power of his own.

At the time of Shaftesbury's trial, John Dryden, the poet laureate, wrote *Absalom and Achitophel*, his greatest satire, as a means of influencing public opinion against the opposition leaders. The poem includes a series of satirical sketches of each of the chief figures in the exclusion controversy. Its description of Buckingham is a masterpiece. Dryden names Buckingham "Zimri" after the Israelite prince who "brought unto his brethren a Midianitish woman in the sight of Moses, and in the sight of all the congregation of the children of Israel, who were weeping before the door of the tabernacle of the congregation" (Num. 25:6). Presumably the name is intended to recall Buckingham's openly adulterous relationship with Lady Shrewsbury. Here is the portrait:

> Some of their Chiefs were Princes of the Land:
> In the first Rank of these did *Zimri* stand:
> A man so various, that he seem'd to be
> Not one, but all Mankinds Epitome.
> Stiff in Opinions, always in the wrong;
> Was every thing by starts, and nothing long:
> But, in the course of one revolving Moon,
> Was Chymist, Fidler, States-Man, and Buffoon:
> Then all for Women, Painting, Rhiming, Drinking;
> Besides ten thousand freaks that dy'd in thinking.
> Blest Madman, who coud every hour employ,
> With something New to wish, or to enjoy!
> Rayling and praising were his usual Theams;
> And both (to shew his Judgment) in Extreams:
> So over Violent, or over Civil,
> That every man, with him, was God or Devil.
> In squandring Wealth was his peculiar Art:
> Nothing went unrewarded but Desert.
> Begger'd by Fools, whom still he found too late:
> He had his Jest, and they had his Estate.
> He laught himself from Court, then sought Releif
> By forming Parties, but coud ne're be Chief:
> For, spight of him, the weight of Business fell
> On *Absalom* and wise *Achitophel*:

Thus, wicked but in will, of means bereft,
He left not Faction, but of that was left.[16]

The portrait is hostile, but it is accurate in pointing out the primary faults of Buckingham's character—his instability, the violence of his affections and hatreds, his extravagance, and his ultimate political ineffectuality.

Retirement and Death

After the end of the Exclusion Crisis, Buckingham retired from public affairs for good. He visited Whitehall only to pay *pro forma* respects to the king, whose displeasure he could no longer afford to risk. In 1685, he published a pamphlet entitled, *A Short Discourse upon the Reasonableness of Men's Having a Religion, or Worship of God*, in which he again argued in favor of religious toleration, the cause to which he was always faithful without hope of success or glory.

In 1686 he retired to his estate in the North Riding of Yorkshire, Castle Helmsley. There he devoted himself to hunting, reading, and directing the operation of his estate. He was now fifty-eight years old. There could be no further chance of political power; Charles, his indulgent master, had died in 1685, and his old enemy, James, duke of York, was now King James II. And his health was failing.

In April of 1687 he contracted a chill from sitting on the damp ground after foxhunting. He went to bed in the house of a tenant, a substantial farmer, at Kirkby Moorside. Though at first he believed his illness was slight, it developed into a high fever. He was destined never to leave the room alive.

On his deathbed he was visited by a cousin, Lord Arran, the future duke of Hamilton. Arran recognized the seriousness of his relative's illness. He spoke seriously to the duke, urging him to make a will and to make his peace with God. Though Buckingham was reluctant to believe that the end was near, he allowed a clergyman to be called. When the parson arrived, he asked the duke "what his Grace's religion was."

"It is an insignificant question," replied Buckingham, "for I have been a shame and disgrace to all religion; if you can do me any good, do."[17]

The sacrament was administered, but Buckingham refused to make a will or to name an heir—whether because he still did not believe he was dying or because he had little property to leave behind, it is now impossible to say. On 16 April 1687, he died. He was buried in an extravagant ceremony at Westminster, paid for by Lord Arran. Of King Charles II and his Cabal, Buckingham was the last to die.

Having been born to great wealth and with great talents, and having expended enormous energy over his lifetime, Buckingham accomplished very little of permanent value. His political career was full of activity but included little real achievement; even the glory he worked so tirelessly to achieve generally evaded him. His open flouting of the rules of conventional morality entertained his companions but exposed him to the scorn of soberer men and to the malice of his enemies.

Most of those who knew him agreed with Bishop Burnet that his greatest gift was his talent for ridicule: "He had the art of treating persons or things in a ridiculous manner beyond any man of the age."[18] With this talent he brought to opposition and satire a congenial mind and ready wit which deserted him when he attempted any serious or positive work. Thus his mockery could topple Clarendon from power and threaten Arlington and Danby, but he could not persuade Parliament or the English people to accept the one great political idea in which he really believed, the toleration of religious dissent. Similarly, his most serious literary works are lifeless and incomplete, whereas his great mock-play, *The Rehearsal*, continues to influence the stage. It is for that work that he most deserves to be remembered today.

Chapter Two
Buckingham's Nondramatic Poetry and Prose

The duke of Buckingham was influenced by, and was a part of, a tradition of courtly writers which originated in the Renaissance. Like Sir Thomas Wyatt in the reign of Henry VIII, Sir Philip Sidney and Sir Walter Raleigh in the time of Queen Elizabeth, and Richard Lovelace and Sir John Suckling in the reign of Charles I, Buckingham thought of himself as a man of affairs first—a politician, a statesman, and a courtier—and a writer second. Because he often wrote to serve his political purposes or to further an intrigue at court, his prose works include speeches delivered in the House of Lords, treatises on policy, and tracts; and most of his nondramatic poems are occasional verse—satires, elegies, complimentary verses, and epigrams, all written in response to particular events.

Buckingham copied much of this occasional verse into his commonplace book. He organized the compositions, both in verse and in prose, under various topics: "Love," "Tears," "House," "Ignoble," and so on. Although the works were written throughout the course of his life, he may have used the book as a means of organizing them—copying from loose papers into the book under the various headings—during his last years of retirement in Yorkshire, for it was found in his pocket after his death. Some of its contents have been published, but they are not readily available; therefore any poems from the commonplace book which are discussed in this chapter will be quoted in full.[1]

Epigrams

An epigram is "a form of writing which makes a satiric, complimentary, or aphoristic observation with wit, extreme condensation, and, above all, brevity."[2] The tradition of writing such poems began

21

with the Greeks; flourished in the hands of the Roman poets Martial and Catullus; descended to such Renaissance poets as Wyatt, Davies, Harington, and Ben Jonson; and was passed from them to the wits of Buckingham's time.[3] Because the epigram is topical and occasional, it is particularly suited for entry in a commonplace book, and most of the poetry in Buckingham's commonplace book is epigrammatic.

The verse form of the epigram is almost always the couplet, but line lengths vary considerably. Although no topic is considered out of bounds, the ideal epigram, according to the eighteenth-century German critic and dramatist Gotthold Lessing, is one which first creates an expectation by calling our attention to some particular subject, then gratifies the expectation by a revelation or explanation.[4] Buckingham's commonplace book contains several epigrams which create such an effect. The following couplet, which appears with several other laments and complaints under the heading "Love" in the commonplace book, is one example: "What strange injustice in my fate doth dwell: / 'Tis she that sins, and I that suffer hell" (80). The first line calls our attention by promising to inform us of a "strange injustice"; the second fulfills the promise and surprises us. The woman's "sin" is her rejection of the lover's suit. If she sinned in another way, by consenting to his suit, he would be released from hell. Thus the word "sin" takes on a new meaning. One sins not by having illicit sexual relations, but by refusing to have them. Because the ordinary meaning of "sin" is the one which first occurs to us when we read the poem, we are momentarily shocked at the reversal of our expectations when we see the word used in this new way. That momentary shock is the reason for the epigram. It gives us a brief, startling opportunity to see things as we have not seen them before.

But not every epigram relies upon paradox to produce its effect. The following epigram, also from the commonplace book, uses hyperbole as its dominant figure: "Some eyes so bright, that they through darkness see. / Where e'er hers come, there can no darkness be" (26). To use hyperbole as the mode of wit in this couplet, Buckingham must make the first part of the epigram hyperbolic in itself. Then the second part must exceed the first by revealing a greater, more surprising hyperbole.

One of Buckingham's contemporaries, the French critic Pierre Nicole, argues in his *Essay on True and Apparent Beauty* against the use of hyperbole in epigram on the grounds that it is inherently false. In his view, to exaggerate matters as hyperbole does is to describe things not as they are, but as we know them not to be.⁵ But Nicole's literalism is simple and narrow. Although hyperbole does not speak the literal truth, it does express a truth of feeling; it says, in effect, that the idea it expresses is felt too deeply for ordinary words to communicate, and that language must be turned against itself, must be pushed to extremes, if the feeling is to be understood. To many seventeenth-century poets, as to the Latin epigrammatists, that truth of feeling is a dominant concern. Donne, for example, in his love lyric "The Relic," concludes, "These miracles we did; but now, alas, / All measure and all language I should pass, / Should I tell what a miracle she was."⁶

For Buckingham in particular, hyperbole was more than a literary figure; it was almost a principle of existence. It suggests the unrestrained, almost maniac energy, intensity, and imagination which characterized him. To be a man of wit was, for him, to be able to see and give expression to the extremes of experience—the compelling beauty of a face, the effortless grace of an action, the outrageous stupidity of a statesman, or the criminal hypocrisy of a king—which other people failed to recognize or to appreciate, or which they lacked the courage, honesty, or ability to express. But to those of a different temperament, Buckingham's extreme reactions seemed foolish and unstable. Thus Dryden, in his portrait of Buckingham in *Absalom and Achitophel*, wrote, "Rayling and praising were his usual theames, / And both (to shew his Judgment) in Extremes."⁷ Dryden's lack of sympathy is apparent; to have a fairer view we might substitute "wit" for "judgment" in his couplet. But he is correct in identifying what might be called Buckingham's "hyperbolic vision" and in perceiving its central importance in his character.

But although hyperbole occurs frequently in Buckingham's epigrams, some of the most successful among them depend on more complex imagery. Buckingham's response to Dryden's portrait of him, for example, uses two interlocking images. It is a poem which the duke wrote and copied into his commonplace book but showed, as far as we know, to no one else:

> To Dryden
>
> As witches images of wax invent
> To torture those they're bid to represent,
> And as the true live substance does decay
> Whilst that slight idol melts in flames away,

> Such, and no lesser, witchcraft wounds my name;
> So thy ill-made resemblance wastes my fame;
> So as the charmed brand consumed i' th' fire,
> So did Meleager's vital heat expire.
> Poor Name! What medicine for thee can I find,
> But thus with stronger charms thy charm t' unbind?
>
> (9)

This poem is both a heartfelt expression of personal pain and a well-crafted epigram. It describes the effect of Dryden's lampoon in two closely related and carefully chosen similes, first that of the witch's idol and second that of Meleager and the burning brand. The image of the wax idol is particularly appropriate, because it recalls the ancient origins of satire in the curse and suggests that modern satire retains something of the magical power it had in antiquity.[8] There may be no logical reason why Dryden's caricature, Zimri, should affect the public perception of Buckingham, any more than there is any logical reason why the witch's victim should sicken and die when the wax image is destroyed—but it happens.

The image of Meleager and the burning brand also alludes to antiquity, to a story from Greek mythology. At Meleager's birth, Atropos, one of the three Fates, prophesied that he would live only as long as the log then burning on the fire was not consumed. His mother, Althaea, snatched the brand from the fire and kept it carefully to insure his life. But years later, after Meleager slew his mother's two brothers, she, in a rage, threw the brand into a fire. As soon as it was consumed, Meleager died. In this simile the brand is not an image of Meleager; it is simply arbitrarily identified with him. But the idea that the destruction of one affects the other reinforces Buckingham's idea, that his reputation is being consumed by the identification of him with Dryden's caricature.

Both images imply that Dryden's language in *Absalom and Achitophel* possesses a power far beyond its mere denotative significance, a power so great that it is almost magical. This is a point which critical exposition could not have made so succinctly, but which such exposition may illustrate. Dryden's use of the word "Zimri" as a name for Buckingham is taken from Numbers 25. According to the biblical story, "Israel abode in Shittim, and the people began to commit whoredom with the daughters of Moab" (25:1). Because of this crime, "the anger of the Lord was kindled against Israel," and God visited a plague upon the Israelites. Moses commanded the judges to appease God's anger by killing the men who joined themselves with the Moabites.

> And behold, one of the children of Israel came and brought unto his brethren a Midianitish woman in the sight of Moses, and in the sight of all the congregation of the children of Israel, who were weeping before the door of the tabernacle of the congregations.
> And when Phinehas, the son of Eleazar, the son of Aaron the priest, saw it, he rose up from among the congregation, and took a javelin in his hand;
> And he went after the man of Israel into the tent, and thrust both of them through, the man of Israel, and the woman through her belly. So the plague was stayed from the children of Israel....
> Now the name of the Israelite that was slain, even that was slain with the Midianitish woman, was Zimri. (Num. 25:6-8, 14)

To seventeenth-century readers, familiar with the Bible, Dryden's use of the name "Zimri" for Buckingham could be counted upon to suggest a series of parallels between the two characters. It suggests that Buckingham's adultery with Lady Shrewsbury, like Zimri's adultery, has been an offense to God, that God in His anger may punish England with some terrible misfortune if England does not punish Buckingham. Perhaps a susceptible reader might be led to identify the plague with which God punished Israel, in which "twenty and four thousand" died (Num. 25:9) with the plague which broke out in London in 1665, in which sixty-eight thousand people were killed. The identification might even suggest that to assassinate Buckingham, as Phinehas killed Zimri, would be a godly act. Since Buckingham's father had been assassinated by a religious fanatic, and since he himself had once narrowly escaped a similar attempt on his life, he could not view such a suggestion as an empty threat.[9]

Of course, all these suggestions hold only insofar as readers identify the biblical Zimri with the contemporary Buckingham. The power of Dryden's image inheres in that identification, just as the power of the witch's spell inheres in her "binding" of the charm, her creation of a magic link between her wax figure and her victim. Therefore Buckingham seeks to "unbind" the charm—to break the magic spell which links him to the evil image. Throughout the poem he has identified poetry with witchcraft, so it is logical that in the concluding couplet he attempts to turn his own charm against the original charm, his poem against Dryden's. This last couplet completes the charm. As the word "thus" in the final line suggests, this poem, the very poem we are reading, is Buckingham's countercharm.

The rhetorical structure of the poem is founded upon the words "as" and "so," which are the logical links of the two similes. These words are used in two slightly different senses. In lines 1 and 3, "as" means "in the same way." That is, the action of Dryden's lampoon on Buckingham's name resembles the action of the witch's fire upon her victim. These instances of "as" correlate with "so" in line 6 to complete the first simile. But in line 7, "as" means "at the same time." Thus as the brand was consumed, Meleager was also consumed. Buckingham merges the two senses of the word, to suggest that a resemblance in effect and simultaneity in time are themselves similar. The phrase "so as" in line 7 adds another link of similarity: the story of Meleager resembles the action of the witch, and both resemble Dryden's lampoon on Buckingham. Dryden's ill-will toward Buckingham resembles the malevolence of the witch, or of Atropos in the classical myth. This complex merging of linkages is Buckingham's own charm. It shows how he could construct an apparently simple epigram to contain a concentrated and relatively sophisticated meaning.

As the image of Meleager suggests, Buckingham used references to classical myth as a means of concentrating meaning. The following complimentary poem demonstrates the degree of concentration which such an allusion can achieve within a limited space:

> Breasts
>
> Such were the breasts at which, when earth was young,
> The shining twins of fair Latona hung.
> Upon such milk their growing godheads fed;
> With such a white their beams were nourished.
>
> (3)

Latona, the daughter of a Titan, was impregnated by Zeus and gave birth to Apollo, the god of the sun, and Artemis, the goddess of the moon. If this poem was written to the countess of Shrewsbury in 1670, during her pregnancy with Buckingham's illegitimate child, it compresses into four lines a hyperbolic compliment to his mistress and a hope for a brilliant child.

Among Buckingham's epigrams are several intended to attack his enemies in court intrigue and others whom for any reason he disliked. The following epigram is one example:

> On the Late Lord Chancellor
>
> To ale, and toasts, and the mirth of a catch,
> And all thy witty disputes with the watch;
> To meat without napkins, and trenchers of bread
> Which in many a quarrel has been flung at thy head;
> To a sack by thy side, and a knife in thy pocket
> In an old sheath that stinks like a candle i' th' socket;
> To thy pleasant walks to Westminster Hall
> In a dirty term, and thy justlings for the wall;
> To thy breakfast in Hell, with black pots by the Tally,
> Thy return in a sculler, and dinner in Ram Alley;
> To the glorious court of the Prince d' Amour,
> Where if thou pretendest to be a Counsellor,
> Thou wouldst even there be but weight and a clog,
> Return, return, thou now State Pettifog.[10]
>
> (7)

This poem describes its object, Heneage Finch, as having the low habits and pleasures of an ordinary attorney. The repetition of the word "to," and especially its association in the first line with "ale, and toasts, and the mirth of a catch," lead the reader to believe that he will be reading a toast. Although he soon becomes aware that the praise is ironic ("Thy witty disputes," "Thy pleasant walks"), he can easily assimilate that recognition to the idea of a toast by assuming that the encomium he is reading is an ironic one. The witty surprise of the epigram comes, therefore, in the final line. Instead of being told to raise his glass to his origins, Finch is ordered to return to them—to go back where he came from.

A few of Buckingham's epigrams reflect his interest in science. These tend to be somewhat more general in application than most of the others. Science could serve as a source of imagery, as in this example: "Love's flame kept in, as dangerous does become / As charcoal fires closed in a narrow room" (31). A charcoal fire indoors is dangerous both because it emits carbon monoxide and because it can, if the room is not ventilated, consume so much of the oxygen in the room that the occupants may suffocate. The simile suggests that love, when suppressed, may both consume and poison whoever conceals it. Science could also provide the basis for a hyperbolic insult:

> Nature ne'er leaps but mounts up by degrees:
> So by plant animals she joins beasts and trees.
> This well-linked chain of ordered entity
> Would have been broke, had nature not made thee.
> Thou makest the chain complete, for until then
> There nothing was betwixt a beast and man.
>   (52)

This epigram uses the concept of the Chain of Being, familiar to scholars of the intellectual history of the Renaissance through the eighteenth century, as a source of wit. One characteristic of the chain is continuity, the idea that there are no gaps in the chain, that each species is adjacent to another species which varies from it only in the minutest degree.[11] The person who is the object of satire in this epigram assures continuity between animals and men: he is the "missing link."

Science could also provide the basis for moral reflection:

> Earth, air, and water we depopulate:
> Wonder not then, man's life's so swiftly fled,
> When by so many deaths he's daily fed.
>   (70)

The epigram suggests a kind of poetic justice in the fact that man, who kills so many other species in order to live, dies so quickly. Knowing what we know today about the relationship between life expectancy and a diet high in animal fat, we may find even more truth in this poem than Buckingham's contemporaries could.

Because of its high degree of concentration and its subjection to the natural cadences of the language, the epigram is one of the most restricted and demanding of English verse forms. Even its greatest masters, such as Herrick, Prior, and Landor, have produced work of uneven quality, and there are many poets whose reputation for epigram must rest upon a single excellent example. Judged by these standards, Buckingham stands not in the first rank of English epigrammatists, but among those whose work continues to deserve reading. The epigram was a form which he found congenial, and when, as in "To Dryden," he concentrates complexity of meaning in a few lines; or when, as in "On the Late Lord Chancellor," he first awakens and then surpasses an expectation, he fulfills the promise of the form and justifies his reputation as a man of wit.

Buckingham's Longer Poems

The distinction between epigrams and longer poems can be made only approximately, for there is little difference between the longest of the former and the shortest of the latter. Buckingham's longer poems, like his epigrams, are often occasional, and his choice of subjects for longer poems ranges as widely as for epigrams. In general, however, the longer poems are less concentrated; a single poem may treat several ideas or examine a single idea from more than one perspective. And unlike the epigrams, the longer poems often respond to or play off against the requirements of a formal genre.

The elegy for Lord General Fairfax. Thomas, third baron Fairfax, was commander in chief of the Parliamentary armies from 1645 to 1650. In June 1650, once the civil wars had ended, he resigned his commission and retired to Nun Appleton House, his estate in Yorkshire. There, in accordance with the ideal of Cincinnatus so much admired in his time, he lived the quiet life of a rural landowner, enjoying the companionship of his wife, Anne; his daughter, Mary; and Mary's tutor, the poet Andrew Marvell.

When Buckingham came to Nun Appleton to court Mary Fairfax in 1657, he contracted an admiration for the retired general which continued throughout his life. No doubt one of the qualities he most admired was Fairfax's willingness to resist the temptations of money, power, and glory—temptations to which Buckingham himself was extremely vulnerable. Not only had the general given up his command at the conclusion of the civil wars, but he also refused any reward for his contribution to the restoration of the monarchy in 1660.[12] He returned once again to Nun Appleton, where he lived quietly for the rest of his life.

After Fairfax died in November 1671, Buckingham wrote an elegy for his father-in-law in the form of an irregular ode—called a "Pindaric" in the title of some of the published versions—of five strophes with a total of 61 lines.[13] The style of the poem is likely to surprise a reader whose expectations are created by the form of the ode or by the word "Pindaric" in its title, for its diction has none of the formality or grandeur which is usually associated with the ode. Rather, the style is plain throughout the poem and descends in some places to homely words or even to slang. The use of such words and phrases as *spy'd* (l. 14), *bragg'd* (l. 19), *polls and braves* (l. 30), and *pudder* (l. 32) takes the style down to the level of ordinary conversation—or below it.[14]

Such a contrast between the formality of the genre and the informality of the style is often a characteristic of burlesque poetry, but this poem is not a burlesque; it is a sincere tribute. In this case, the contrast between style and form awakens our attention to many other contrasts in the poem. For the epitaph on Lord Fairfax is a poem about contrast: it uses contrast as a rhetorical technique to treat its subject, which is contrast as a principle of character.

According to the poem, General Fairfax united in his personality several contrasting qualities. He combined extremes of courage and aggressiveness with extremes of gentleness and modesty: "Both sexes virtues were in him combin'd, / He had the fierceness of the manliest mind, / And yet the meekness too of woman-kind" (ll. 5–7). A second contrast exists between Fairfax and baser men, who lack both his courage and his humility. Whereas they boast of their courage and ferocity even in defeat, Fairfax blushed at the mention of his successes (ll. 19–22). Whereas other men put on the appearance of greatness even if they cannot attain the substance of it, Fairfax achieved the reality of greatness while retaining the plainness, simplicity, and unselfishness of his life.

A third contrast is only partly explicit. It is the contrast between Fairfax, who could have had power but renounced it, and the many men who spend their lives struggling for power. Many of the seekers after power are simply fools or knaves, "Who such a pudder make / Through dulness and mistake / In seeking after pow'r, and get it not" (ll. 32–34). These men may be irritating, but they are not dangerous. A more serious threat is posed by those who have the ability to gain power combined with the lust to achieve it. Here Buckingham creates an implicit contrast between Fairfax and Oliver Cromwell, Fairfax's associate in the command of the Parliamentary armies, who, when Fairfax retired in 1650, assumed full command and went on to become the conqueror of Scotland, to dismiss the Parliament, and to rule England as a dictator. The power which Cromwell seized, Buckingham tells us, could have belonged to Fairfax:

> He might have been a king,
> But that he understood
> How much it was a meaner thing
> To be unjustly great, than honourably good.
> (ll. 49–52)

The poem shows that Fairfax's simplicity and modesty were and are not simply a matter of personal taste and private ethics, but a political principle.[15]

A pivotal element in Buckingham's exposition of this theme is the word *great*, which is used in the poem in two distinct senses. In the phrase "unjustly great," quoted above, *great* means "eminent," "important," or "powerful." In the following lines, however, the word moves to quite a different meaning:

> Through his whole life, the part he bore
> Was wonderful and great,
> And yet it so appear'd in nothing more,
> Than in his private last retreat;
> (ll. 23–26)

In line 24, *great* means "critical"—important in its significance. But in lines 25–26 *great* takes on a new meaning; it now means "magnanimous" or "noble"—having a lofty soul. Fairfax's nobility of mind, concealed by the simplicity and modesty of his personal character, is seen to be of a far greater quality than the emptiness or ruthlessness of other men, concealed by the external splendor of their titles and honors.

Thus what at first seems to be a confusion or misalignment of style and form is in fact a resolution of such a confusion. Buckingham's elegy teaches us to call things by their proper names and to distrust the grandeur of conventional forms. Those whom we are accustomed to thinking of as "great men" because they have the adulation of the multitude and the trappings of power may in fact be "mean" (l. 51) if their greatness is founded on injustice. And not only is nobility compatible with plainness, but plainness may be, in itself, the highest kind of nobility when plainness is chosen consciously by one who has the power to choose.

Similarly, we are accustomed to thinking of the Pindaric ode as "great" (it is sometimes called the "great ode") because of the heroic style in which it is written. The diction applied to Fairfax throughout this poem is unremarkable either for elevation or the lack of it; like the man, it is simple and plain but rich in hidden meaning. The words cited above as low or slang all occur in descriptions of the vainglorious men to whom Fairfax is contrasted. Thus Buckingham aligns his style not with the genre but with the subject—the plain with the plain, the low with the low—and achieves a true nobility of theme.

Some love poetry. Only a few of Buckingham's longer poems deserve the title of love poems. They include poems entitled "Love" and "Epithalamium" in the commonplace book and poems entitled "To His Mistress" and "The Lost Mistress: A Complaint against the Countess of ———" in his published works.[16]

As their titles indicate, these are fairly conventional poems. "The Lost Mistress" records the complaint of a shepherd who, deserted by the woman he loves, is torn between his desire to give voice to his pain and his reluctance to speak ill of the woman whom he still loves, despite the injury she has done him. "To His Mistress" is addressed by the speaker to the woman he loves; he tells her that he never could have loved her if it were not for her superior mind and noble soul, but he is also racked with desire for her body. "Love" describes the pain of one who loves unrequitedly and who sees all around him in nature the fulfillment of love. And the "Epithalamium" is the celebration of a marriage, the fulfillment of love.

Perhaps the most noticeable characteristic of Buckingham's love poetry is his awareness of nature and the degree to which it shares the lover's mood. As noted above, one of the poems is devoted entirely to that idea:

Love

Season of joy, and of delight,
    To all the world but me;
  I only am excluded quite
From Nature's universal jollity.
The plants and flowers look upwards and admire
    The sun their beauteous sire;
    The sun does every day
With his green smiling infants love to play.
Hark, how the birds now tune their wondrous throats;
    Nature needs more to hear
    Music's most ravishing notes,
For every bough does his own Orpheus bear.

> Well may the birds sing and rejoice,
> Since all have made their happy choice.
> Since of all birds that be,
> There's not one false or one disdainful she.

The first four lines of the poem inform us that the speaker does not share the universal happiness of spring, but we do not discover why until we reach the final line—though we may well guess, since poems with this theme are fairly common. One less conventional element in the poem is that the rejoicing and adoration which the speaker sees in nature are not, for most of the length of the poem, those of mating. The plants and flowers adore not one another, but "the sun their beauteous sire," and the birds seem to be enjoying a relationship not with one another, but with the tree branches. It is only in the last three lines that the mutuality of the love of birds is contrasted with the disappointments of human love.

A slightly more complex treatment of the same theme can be seen in "The Lost Mistress," where nature seems to share the unhappy lover's pain:

> Forsaken Strephon in a lonesome glade,
> By nature for despairing sorrows made,
> Beneath a blasted oak had laid him down,
> By light'ning that, as he by love o'erthrown.
> Upon a mossy root he lean'd his head,
> While at his feet a murmuring current lead
> Her streams, that sympathiz'd with his sad moans;
> The neighb'ring echoes answer'd all his groans.
> Then as the dewy morn restor'd the day,
> Whilst stretch'd on earth the silent mourner lay,
> At last into these doleful sounds he broke,
> Obdurate rocks dissolving whilst he spoke.

Whereas the conventionality of "Love" makes its statements about nature somewhat unexciting, the use of the third-person narrator in these lines creates a greater problem. In "Love" it is the perception of the scorned lover that all of nature enjoys loving interrelationships. Readers need not believe that nature really does participate in such relationships; we need believe only that a man who has been scorned by the woman he loves may think so. In "The Lost Mistress," however, the narrative (at least in the opening and closing sections) is in the third person, and we are implicitly asked to believe that the sympathy between Strephon and nature is perceived not just by Strephon himself, but by the narrator.

At first the relationship seems merely fortuitous; Strephon happens to have chosen for his repose a spot which seems to be in sympathy with him. The place is "By nature for despairing sorrows made" because it contains a tree overthrown by lightning, a mossy root, a murmuring stream, and an echo. All these things occur naturally enough and may reasonably be supposed to coexist in many places; only in the human mind does any connection between them and Strephon's state of mind exist. But when we are told in line 10 that "Obdurate rocks dissolv[ed] whilst he spoke," we have a new situation. Now we are told of something which cannot possibly happen—and we are told it as if it were fact. Occurring where it does, surrounded by statements of fact, this statement is impossible for a reader to accept; consequently it is a flaw in the poem.

Buckingham's most successful treatment of the imaginative interaction between nature and the perceptions of the lover occurs in his "Epithalamium," where the eye of the narrator in the opening strophe sees the dawn, Aurora, as a beautiful bride being dressed by her attendants. The entire poem follows:

> By her the gentle hours attending stand
> And dress the bridal morn with skilful hand.
> Her fairest robes of silver light she wears;
> With comely art they comb her golden hairs.
> An orient pendant Hesper she puts on,
> With beauty all, and beauteous riches shown
> Never so bright and gay, since she was led
> By the kind hours to loved Tithonus' bed.
>   Ah, cruel youth, who fiercely dost invade,
> And from her parents snatch the trembling maid!
> Thou like a tyrant with a conqueror's claim
> Dost give new laws, and change her very name,
> Riflest her beauties and her virgin store:
> In cities took by storm they do no more.
>   Kind youth, whose love swells to so large a space,
> It fills the brother's, father's, mother's place!
>   I saw his years like trees well ranged stand
> In a long row, and hers on th' other hand;
> With comely kindness their fair tops they twined,
> Beauty and pleasure in their shades combined.

> A thousand winged Cupids, bright and young,
> Like swarms of bees upon the branches hung.
> Both sides did to an equal length extend;
> Both sides were green and flourishing to the end.

The classical personifications of Aurora, Tithonus, and Hesper which Buckingham uses in his first strophe are a particularly effective way of suggesting union between man and nature. Tithonus, according to Greek myth, was a mortal youth beloved by Aurora, goddess of the dawn. To make him her lover, the goddess secured for him eternal life, but she neglected to ask for eternal youth, so that Tithonus becomes perpetually older while the goddess remains forever young. Hesperus, the evening star, is the planet Venus. Edmund Spenser, in his *Epithalamion* (1595), had used the same classical personifications.[17] But Buckingham's combining the images into a beautiful and consistent metaphor is original with him, and it is one of the most successful images anywhere in his poetry. Here, as in Spenser's poem, we are asked to see the natural world in a kind of marriage with the mind and mood of the lover—not to see impossible sights, as in "The Lost Mistress," but to see reality through the eye of metaphor.

The final strophe, in which the years of the bridal couple's future are seen as two parallel rows of trees with their branches joined to form an arch, reverses the imagery of the opening section. In the opening lines nature is personified; here human life is shown as a natural scene. Unlike Aurora and Tithonus, whose inequality must increase with each new day, this wedding couple will be equally long-lived, equally fresh and flourishing. It is a beautiful image, and the addition of the cupids as bees is a happy piece of baroque detail.

The two central strophes, in which the bridegroom is first called "cruel" because he takes his bride from her family and then "kind" because he replaces their love with his own, turn on verbal conceits rather than natural imagery. They are not as satisfying as the opening and closing sections. But it is clear that Buckingham planned the poem as a symmetrical whole, as the following outline illustrates: strophe 1: nature as human; strophe 2: bridegroom as cruel; strophe 3: bridegroom as kind; strophe 4: man's life as nature. The poem thus completes its own circle, even more effectively than "To Dryden" does. Despite the weakness of the central section, this is one of Buckingham's best and most moving poems.

The least successful of Buckingham's love poems is "To His Mistress." Written in forty-four lines of varying lengths and rhyme schemes, it turns on the same kind of rhetorical contrasts which work so well in the elegy for lord general Fairfax. The mistress is contrasted in the first twelve lines with the speaker's previous loves—women whom, he now realizes, he never really loved. In the second section (ll. 13–27), the speaker explains why he has never loved until now: he lists the criteria for a woman who is to create true love in a man with "a discerning eye." These requirements, of course, compliment not only the mistress, who has met them, but also the speaker himself, who must be assumed to have the "discerning eye" which can appreciate them. Not only must the lady have "looks and shape," but she must have "wit and judgment," "greatness of thought and worth," "plainness and truth" (ll. 19–20, 26). If she has all these qualities, she will "beget a passion for her mind"—that is, cause a man to fall in love with her mind rather than her body. Having listed these qualities and their effects, the speaker discovers that only the lady addressed can meet the requirements:

> She must be—what said I? she must be you,
> None but yourself that miracle can do;
> At least, I'm sure, thus much I plainly see,
> None but yourself e'er did it upon me:
> (ll. 28–31)

The broken construction in line 28 and the qualification in line 30 seem intended to give the effect of present thought—that is, to show the mind of the speaker as he interrupts one thought to amend it with another. The most striking instance of such an interruption comes in line 37, where, having spent twenty-four lines explaining the importance of a noble mind to true love, the speaker bursts into an eruption of passion for the woman's body:

> But oh! your body too is divine,
> I kill myself with wishing you all mine.
> In pain and anguish, night and day,
> I faint, and melt away:
> (ll. 37–40)

In its theme, therefore, "To His Mistress" is somewhat similar to Donne's "The Ecstasy." In both works an attraction of mind and soul is the basis for love, but the attraction of the body is acknowledged to be powerful, to be the basis of the higher passion, and to be valuable in itself. In both poems dramatic immediacy is created by the interruption of one absolute statement with another. Yet whereas "The Ecstasy" is one of the greatest love poems of the seventeenth century, "To His Mistress" is a failure and a disappointment.

There are two main reasons for this failure. One is the fact that the speaker's listing his requirements for a perfect love makes him seem self-satisfied and superior. Instead of being overcome with passion, the speaker seems to be making out a shopping list. Instead of describing the mutuality of attraction which is necessary to love, he seems to be interested primarily in himself, and in the woman only as someone who can meet his requirements:

> She, that would raise a noble love, must find
> Ways to beget a passion for her mind;
> She must be that, which she to be would seem;
> For all true Love is grounded on esteem:
> (ll. 22–25)

The other problem with the poem is that its ideas seem so fixed and its expressions so conventional that the impression of dramatic immediacy is not really created. Phrases like "I kill myself with wishing you all mine," and "I faint and melt away," and even the exclamation, "But oh!" are all drawn from the battery of conventional expressions used by most amatory poets. Consequently the poem lacks the freshness and sincerity that it labors to create.

And yet it is possible that Buckingham actually wrote this poem to his mistress, Lady Shrewsbury, and that it is completely sincere. The qualities of nobility of mind and of plainness and truth which the speaker values in his mistress are the same qualities which Buckingham celebrated in Lord Fairfax. But however unsteady Buckingham's wit may have been, however many times it may have missed fire, it was a more reliable source of poetic excellence than his ideas and feelings plainly stated.

Personal satires. The poetry of personal attack has existed at least since ancient Greece, and several Elizabethan poets produced effective examples of it. But in the Restoration personal satires became both more numerous and more virulent than ever before, at least in English. Some of the writers may have been moved, as they claimed, by moral or political principle, but many others wrote with simple malice, or destroyed a reputation to promote an intrigue. No one, from King Charles to the most ordinary prostitute, was free from attack. The poems circulated in manuscript and were published, if at all, many years after the events which prompted them.

Buckingham's personal satires avoid the most unethical practices of his contemporaries. Whereas many of the anonymous satires are gossipy "shotgun lampoons," besmirching the reputation of one person after another, his libels are almost always directed primarily against single individuals; subsidiary characters are included only because of their association with the primary target. Whereas many contemporary satirists attacked easy targets like the "court ladies" and ascribed to them real or fancied deviant sexual practices, Buckingham attacked only those he believed had injured him or his friends, and he never mentioned the sexual behavior of his victims.[18]

As the epigram on Heneage Finch, discussed earlier, illustrates, Buckingham's personal satires concentrate on the physical characteristics and personal habits of the person under attack. He seems most to be offended by an association with sordid or ignoble persons, places, or habits, and by a lack of *savoir-faire*.

For example, in his "Advice to a Painter to Draw my Lord Arlington, Grand Minister of State," Buckingham suggests that Arlington's physical characteristics can show us the qualities of his mind:

> First draw an arrant fop, from top to toe,
> Whose very looks at first dash shew him so:
> Give him a mean proud garb, a dapper face,
> A pert dull grin, a black patch cross his face;
> Two goggle-eyes, so clear, tho' very dead,
> That one may see, thro' them, quite thro' his head.
> (ll. 1–6)

And in his "Familiar Epistle to Mr. Julian, Secretary to the Muses," he suggests that Sir Carr Scroope's red face somehow indicates an exclusion from human fellowship:

> Of his unfinished face what shall I say,
> But that 'twas made of Adam's own red clay,
> That much, much ochre was on it bestow'd:
> God's image 'tis not, but some Indian god.
> (ll. 30–33)[19]

Like most lampooners, Buckingham constructs a caricature of his victim, a portrait enough like him to be recognizable but sufficiently exaggerated and ridiculous to be insulting. As part of the caricature, he attributes to the victim extravagant characteristic actions. In the "Epistle to Julian" Buckingham describes Scroope as an incorrigible poet, unable to restrain himself from writing verse:

> For when his passion has been bubbling long,
> The scum at last boils up into a song,
> And sure no mortal creature at one time
> Was e'er so far o'ergone with love and rhyme.
> To his dear self of poetry he talks:
> His hands and feet are scanning as he walks.
>   (ll. 51–56)

In the lampoon on Arlington, Buckingham attacks both Arlington's gravity of manner and the folly which lies under that gravity by describing the minister playing with his daughter:

> Next all his implements of folly draw,
> His iv'ry-staff, his snuff-box, and Tatta,[20]
> That pretty babe, that makes his lordship glad,
> And all the company besides so sad;
> She who in state is brought, to smoothe his brow,
> When he has rul'd the roast, the Lord knows how,
> For tho' to us he's stately like a king,
> He'll joke and droll with her like any thing.
>   (ll. 11–18)

The most imaginative of Buckingham's personal satires is the one entitled "Upon the Installment of Sir [Thomas] Os[bor]n, and the late Duke of Newcastle." The event which the poem commemorates is the installation of the two title characters as members of the Order of the Garter at Windsor Castle on 19 April 1677. Although Buckingham was a member of the Order, he was not present at the ceremony; at the instigation of Osborne (the lord treasurer, now properly called the earl of Danby) he and three other Whig leaders had been imprisoned in the Tower of London. Since Buckingham had sponsored Osborne's rise to power, he deeply resented the ingratitude of his former protégé.

Like Buckingham's other lampoons, this one describes the personal characteristics of the victim: Osborne is thin and pale and has a foul breath. He is subject to the control of his eccentric wife. But whereas in most of the personal satires the tone is coolly detached or archly amused, calling our attention to the victim as a mere curiosity, this poem has at its core a passage of pure invective in which we recognize the tone of *saeva indignatio* ("savage indignation") which is the emotional pitch of the most powerful satire.

That tone is introduced to the poem by the appearance of a new speaker, St. George, the patron saint of the Order of the Garter. The saint appears at the ceremony in disguise, inquires what is going on, and passes judgment on the candidates for installation. He recognizes that Newcastle is "an ass, / But for his father's sake, he let him pass." (Newcastle's father, who had fought many battles and made great financial sacrifices for the crown during the civil wars, was known as "The Loyal Duke.") But St. George angrily rebuffs Osborne:

> How dare you in this chapel keep a quarter,
> With your blue lips, bluer than robes or garter?
> Go get a shroud to match your face and breath,
> Be drest, as well as look and smell, like death.
> (ll. 60–63)

This is the only one of Buckingham's personal satires in which a visionary or allegorical character appears. St. George is to this poem what the images of witchcraft are to "To Dryden" and the natural imagery is to "Epithalamium": an imaginative means of compressing meaning and achieving elevation of tone.

Taken together as the work of a lifetime, Buckingham's poems are not very numerous. They are the productions of a man of wit, learning, and taste who sometimes wrote poetry, not of a professional poet. Several of his poems, like "To His Mistress" or the "Epistle to Julian," are merely conventional. But when, as in the elegy for Fairfax, he brings us to a new understanding of what we thought we knew, or when, as in "To Dryden" or "Epithalamium," he creates images which surprise and move us, we recognize that he was not limited to the conventional. If Buckingham was an amateur in poetry, he was a gifted amateur.

Major Prose Works

A Letter to Sir Thomas Osborn on Reading a Book called The Present Interest of England Stated (1672). In 1672, England declared war on Holland, as it had promised to do in the Treaty of Dover, signed with France in 1670. Buckingham, as a member of the Cabal ministry and as the chief negotiator of the public version of that treaty, supported the war. But the war was not popular with the English public, to whom the Dutch seemed not enemies but natural allies. Like England, Holland was a small Protestant country, threatened by the power of France; and like England, Holland was dependent on international trade for its prosperity. England, moreover, had pledged itself in the Triple Alliance, signed in 1668 by England, Sweden, and Holland, to aid the Dutch if they were attacked by the French, so that the declaration of war seemed a breach of faith.

Arguments against the war were made everywhere—in the press, in Parliament, and in the streets. Among many other publications against the war was a pamphlet, anonymously published, entitled *The Present Interest of England Stated.* Buckingham, looking for a way to state the ministry's side of the case, decided to write a private letter, addressed to Sir Thomas Osborne, who in 1672 was still his protégé in the government, in which he could argue against the pamphlet. His letter could then be published.

The *Letter* has a three-part organization. In the first section Buckingham argues that England should look after her own interests. It might be true that England and Holland have much in common, but England should not let feelings of kinship or solidarity blind her to her own interests. In the second section Buckingham considers the terms of the Triple Alliance, trying to show that the alliance does not bar England from joining forces with France to make war on Holland. In the third section he attempts to demonstrate that Holland poses a threat to England.

Buckingham's point that England's interest leads inevitably to conflict with Holland has as its premise the idea that the two nations are rivals in trade. "Had the author [of the anonymous pamphlet] been a lover, instead of a politician, he would have known, that rivals are the things in this world, which men commonly do, and ought most to hate," he wrote.[21] His analogy between rivalries in love and those in trade is witty and effective; it suggests that whereas the author of the *Present Interest* is a narrow student of statecraft, Buckingham is a man of the world. But the analogy may not necessarily hold. Rivals in love contend for the love of one woman. When she accepts one, she must spurn the other. But rivals in trade may create more trade for both, since a thriving international trade enriches all who participate in it.

Although Buckingham does not extend his analogy, the kind of thinking that produces it appears everywhere in the *Letter*. Thus just as a jealous lover might fear and resent the virtues of his rival as threats to his success, Buckingham suggests that the English ought to fear the virtues of the Dutch: "The true aim of every Englishman should be the good and prosperity of England; for that reason, industry and parsimony are to be wished for in the inhabitants of England, because they are qualities advantageous for us, and useful to our trade: but for the same reason, they ought not by us to be wished for in the inhabitants of Holland, because those qualities in them are prejudicial to England, and destructive to our trade" (166). However logical these arguments may be, they strike us today as mean-spirited. In either love or trade, a magnanimous suitor would rather succeed by virtue of his own good qualities than by wishing away those of his rival.

To the argument that the Triple Alliance forbids an attack on Holland, Buckingham opposes a legalistic analysis of the occasion and terms of that alliance. The Alliance had been set up in 1668 to counter the advance of the French armies into the Spanish Netherlands. The parties to the alliance pledged not only to oppose France, but to come to the aid of one another if France attacked them. Now France had attacked Holland—but England had joined France. In Buckingham's view this change of policy was justified by a change in England's interest: "self-preservation ought to be looked after a little in these kind of affairs: and ... if the consequence of the loss of Flanders did not somewhat concern us, we should be no more in pain about it than we were for the conquest of Granada" (170). Splitting hairs very precisely, Buckingham argues that although the Triple Alliance binds England to protect Flanders from France, it does not bind England not to attack Holland. He heaps ridicule on the suggestion that the first of these propositions implies the second:

This, under favour, is an absurdity yet greater than the former, there being no one thing you can allege as a consequence to any other thing whatsover, that will not make every whit as sensible a conclusion as this. For example, to say, you ought not to go to bed to night, because the King of Spain did not go yesterday a hunting; or that I must not dine to morrow because Monsieur de Wit loves dancing, is not a more incoherent discourse, than that, because we have promised with the Dutch to save Flanders from the French, therefore what injuries soever the Dutch shall offer us, we cannot defend ourselves against them. The argument, if you mark it, is just thus, that because I agree with William to save Thomas, therefore I am bound to let William cut my throat. (170)

Of course, the argument is not so ridiculous as Buckingham pretends. England had promised not only to protect Flanders, but to aid Holland if she were attacked by France. But Buckingham insists that the Triple Alliance requires England to aid Holland only if she is attacked by France as a consequence of her having joined the Triple Alliance (168), and not if she is attacked on any other pretext whatsoever. Although his reading of the terms of the alliance may be legally correct, certainly he is one of the first statesmen ever to argue that a declaration of war upon an ally is not a breach of the alliance!

A key phrase buried in the quotation above is "what injuries soever the Dutch shall offer us." England might be justified in making war on Holland despite the Triple Alliance if the Dutch have in some way injured the English. In the third section of the *Letter* Buckingham asserts three types of injury. First, he writes, "it has been their constant practice to massacre and make slaves of our countrymen in the East Indies" (166). This allegation is a reference to the Massacre of Amboyna (1623), in which the Dutch East India Company in the Spice Islands (modern Indonesia) drove out the English East India Company. Second, Buckingham asserts that the Dutch "rob us of our trade" (175). This statement takes for granted that the trade routes are the propery of the English, which the Dutch are stealing from them, rather than that the two countries have equal right to the freedom of the seas. Finally, Buckingham argues, in a far-fetched scenario, that the Dutch might combine forces with the French to conquer England (171–74). To support this idea requires particularly strained reasoning: "To this it is objected, that it can never be the interest of Holland to join with France in the conquest of England; but for aught we know they may mistake their interest;

and certainly it is not wisdom in any nation, to have its safety depend upon the prudence of another" (172). Of these three reasons, only the first will stand even the most casual scrutiny by any disinterested observer. The Amboyna massacre was real. But although the trading wars between the English and Dutch East India Companies were conducted without much compassion on either side, there had been no provocation from the Dutch in fifty years.

The *Letter to Sir Thomas Osborn* is not a rhetorical success. Its arguments are so strained that they could appeal only to a reader who was predisposed to agree with them, and in the political climate of the time, such readers were not very numerous. It displays, in its analogies, a little of Buckingham's characteristic wit and energy, but in general it is unworthy of its author.

***The Short Discourse Upon the Reasonableness of Men's Having a Religion, or Worship of God* (1685).** Buckingham's *Short Discourse* must have been written fairly early in 1685, probably in the early spring.[22] Although it appears at first to be a philosophical or theological treatise, it is primarily a political tract, an attempt to win adherents to the idea of religious toleration, the political principle to which Buckingham was most constantly faithful.

To see Buckingham's *Discourse* in its context, we must begin by recognizing that in the seventeenth century every religious idea was a political idea. England contained three major Christian groups: Roman Catholics, members of the Church of England, and Protestants outside the Church of England (including Presbyterians, Baptists, Quakers, and many others), broadly called Dissenters. For over a century these three groups had struggled to control the faith of their countrymen and the government of the nation. To the Anglicans, Roman Catholicism was identified with the reign of "Bloody Mary" Tudor in the 1550s and the martyrdom of Anglican bishops, with the Gunpowder Plot of Guy Fawkes and his accomplices to blow up Parliament and seize control of the government in 1605, and with the French tyranny of Louis XIV in their own time. The Dissenters were associated in the Anglican mind with the Parliamentary side in the Civil War, with the execution of King Charles I in 1649, and with the dictatorship of Oliver Cromwell. The Test Act (1673), which prohibited anyone except a member of the Church of England from holding any office in the government or universities, suggests the prevailing level of religious tolerance. It was nearly impossible for most seventeenth-century Englishmen to imagine a commonwealth in which each person was free to worship as he pleased, without interference from others and without interfering with the rights of others himself.

But for Buckingham, such a commonwealth was the natural extension of British liberty. In 1675, in a speech in the House of Lords to prepare the way for a Bill of Indulgence (i.e., a bill to grant religious freedom) for Protestant dissenters, he reasoned that religious persecution was a serious political mistake because "it makes every man's safety depend upon the wrong place, not upon the Governors, or man's living well towards the Civil Government, established by Law; but upon his being transported with Zeal for every opinion that's held by those that have power in the Church that's in fashion."[23] The sarcastic tone of "transported with Zeal" and "the Church that's in fashion" could have done his cause little good. The bill was defeated.

In 1674, in a letter to his friend and secretary, Martin Clifford, Buckingham expressed himself in much franker terms. Almost as if he were an antireligious polemicist, he asserts here that the behavior of religious zealots can make religion itself an evil:

> This has made each party such enemies to moderation and liberty of conscience, when it got to the helm; which if once justly and firmly established, would open the door to that peace, which the gospel was bestowed on us to introduce into the world. Lucretius, from his reflection on the sacrificing of Iphigenia for a wind at Aulis, forms his celebrated epiphonema:
>
> *Tantum Religio potuit suadere malorum.*[24]
>
> But what would he have said, if he had lived after the establishment of the Christian religion, and seen the heats and animosities betwixt the Arians and Orthodox, or the several opinions that started up amongst them, when once the heathen folly was sunk and removed, and power had debauched the principle, which Christ gave as the characteristic of his disciples, "the love of one another." If he had seen how many millions of men lost their lives, in the contests about the supremacy of the popes; and the quarrels betwixt the emperors, and the bishops of Rome; or the one and twenty millions destroyed by the Spaniards in the reduction of the West-Indies.... If he had known the noble methods of the inquisition of the romanists, and the penal laws of the reformed, by which in our nation alone, in a few years, three-score thousand families were ruined, he would have been no longer amazed at the sacrificing one poor greensickness girl.[25]

The rhetorical force of these sentences anticipates some of the greatest effects produced by Swift. The rising energy of the successive clauses, the suspension of the "If" clause to build anticipation, the statistics of millions of lives lost, the scornful irony of "noble methods," and the crowning contemptuous phrase, "one poor green-sickness girl"—each contributes to the power of the whole. Buckingham's indignation here at the wickedness and stupidity of the human race is the *saeva indignatio* of the true satirist.

The decade following the letter to Martin Clifford was filled with political crises in which religious controversy played a prominent part— the Exclusion Crisis, the Rye House Plot, and others—and in the spring of 1685, there was a new threat to freedom of conscience. With the accession of King James II to the throne after his brother's death, England had an openly Catholic king for the first time since Mary Tudor. The possibility that James would ally himself with the High-Church Tories to persecute the Dissenters seemed very strong. And Buckingham, now living in retirement in Yorkshire, no longer exercised any political power, even in opposition. If he were to influence public affairs, it must be by persuading public opinion.

But the means of persuasion could not be rational argument. After years of failure to advance the cause of religious toleration by means of reason, Buckingham had lost faith in its power, at least in religious controversy: "The world is made up for the most part of fools and knaves, both irreconcilable foes to truth: the first being slaves to a blind credulity, which we may properly call bigotry: the last are too jealous of that power, they have usurp'd over the folly and ignorance of the others, which the establishment of the empire of reason would destroy" (Letter to Martin Clifford, 176). In the *Short Discourse*, therefore, Buckingham proceeds by means of a kind of rhetorical entrapment of his reader. Although the essay is, at its core, a plea for religious toleration, it begins, or at least pretends to begin, as a rational defense of Christianity against atheism. And although it pretends to be a series of logical deductions, each leading inevitably from the previous one, it actually uses the appearance of logic to confuse its reader and to entrap him into assent.

In the message entitled "To the Reader" which prefaces the *Discourse*, Buckingham puts his reader off guard by confounding a probable expectation: "When I began to write upon this Subject, it was out of a Curiosity I had to try, what I could say, in reason, against the bold Assertions of those Men, who think it a witty thing to defame

Religion." A reader aware of Buckingham's reputation as a witty and irreligious man[26] might be led by the full title of the *Discourse* to expect logical arguments against religion. Instead he finds Buckingham allying himself with the religious against the witty and profane. In addition, however, Buckingham tells his reader that the train of reasoning in the work has taken an inevitable direction: "By the nature of this Discourse, I was forced to Conclude with an Opinion, which I have been long convinced of; That nothing can be more Anti-Christian, nor more contrary to Sense and Reason, than to Trouble and Molest our Fellow-Christians, because they cannot be exactly of our Minds, in all the things relating to the Worship of God." That is, the logic of the discourse, operating with a kind of life of its own, forced the conclusion. The suggestion is that a tolerance of religious differences is the necessary consequence of any reasonable discussion of the nature of religion itself.

To understand the way the *Discourse* affects its reader, we need to keep in mind the fact that literature is a kinetic art—that it influences the ideas and feelings of its readers in time, as they progress through the work.[27] Thus the lengthy opening sentence, which seems only to delay the main subject of the work, in fact promotes its most important effect:

> There is nothing that gives Men a greater dissatisfaction, than to find themselves disappointed in their Expectations; especially of those things in which they think themselves most concern'd; and therefore all, who go about to give Demonstrations, in Matters of Religion, and fail in the attempt, do not only leave Men less Devout than they were before, but also, with great pains and industry, lay in their Minds the very Grounds and Foundations of Atheism: For the generality of Mankind, either out of laziness, or a diffidence of their being able to judge aright in Points that are not very clear, are apt rather to take things upon trust than to give themselves the trouble to examine whether they be true or no. (1–2)[28]

The ostensible purpose of the opening sentence is to explain why Buckingham intends to rely upon probabilities, rather than to attempt to demonstrate his ideas with absolute certainty. But that explanation is not completed until the next paragraph. The immediate effect of the sentence is subtly to plant doubt about the idea of certainty in religion, for it suggests that most religious beliefs are founded on habit, laziness, and ignorance, and that an examination of them more often raises doubt than provides confirmation. In the second paragraph, apparently still commenting upon his methods, Buckingham says that he will content himself with establishing probability "Because, if I can convince a Man, that the Notions I maintain are more likely to be True than False, it is not in his power not to believe them; no Man believing any thing because he has a mind to believe it, but because his Judgment is convinc'd, and he cannot choose but believe it, whether he will nor no" (3). By pointing out that belief is not an act of will, Buckingham again anticipates his conclusion and undermines a reader's belief that he is in possession of truth and has the right to force others to accept it.

After more comments on the nature of belief and conviction and more stipulations on his mode of procedure, Buckingham appears to get to the start of his central argument: "The first main Question, upon the clearing of which I shall endeavour to ground the Reasonableness of Men's having a Religion, or Worship of God, is this, Whether it is more probable that the World has ordered itself to be in the Form it now is, or was contriv'd to be so by some other Being of a more perfect, and more designing nature?" (5). But a reader who expects now to settle down to a smoothly developing argument is immediately disappointed, for in the act of dismissing a secondary question, Buckingham follows it: "For whether or no the World has been Created out of nothing, is not material to our purpose.... Yet because this latter Question ought not to be totally pass'd by, I shall take the liberty to offer some Conceptions of mine upon it" (5). There then follow four pages of argument on that question. When Buckingham returns to his original question, he restates it in a somewhat altered form: "Whether it be more probable, that the World, or that God Almighty has been from all Eternity?" (9).

Now Buckingham's reasoning begins to move more quickly. Because the world changes constantly, he reasons that God, who is unchanging, must be more likely to be eternal than the world. Obviously he has begged the question: in an argument intended to establish whether or not God exists, he has used an alleged attribute of God as evidence of His existence. If God does not exist, He is not eternally unchanging.

Next, Buckingham asks whether God cares more for human beings than for other animals. Unsurprisingly, his answer is that God prefers humans. The reason for God's preference establishes the next link in Buckingham's chain of reasoning: "There is something nearer a-kin to the Nature of God in Men, than there is in any other Animals whatsoever" (11–12). This godly element in human nature is the soul and the reasoning faculty or will. As Buckingham sees it, the two are one: "an Eternal Being, and Free-will, are things in their Nature inseparable one from the other."

This "Instinct of God," another name Buckingham gives to this godly element, must tell us how to behave toward God—in other words, must be our guide to religious truth. "That Religion is probably the best, whose Doctrine does most recommend to us those Things, which, by that Instinct, we are prompted to believe are Vertues, and good Qualities: And that, I think, without exceeding the Bounds of Modesty, I may take upon me to affirm, Is the Christian Religion" (18). Here there is hardly even the pretense of logical argument. By the standard of belief Buckingham proposes, a case could be made for any major organized religion. But this deficiency of logic is no fault from the point of view of the real purpose of the *Discourse*. The reader is being told that his own beliefs are those which most perfectly suit the nature of God and man. To the degree that he believes what he is told, he will accept the idea that he is following a logical argument, and he will be disposed to accept the conclusion that Buckingham has already foreshadowed in his foreword—that the necessity of religious toleration follows inevitably from logical reasoning about religion. To the degree that the reader doubts Buckingham's assertions or feels uncomfortable with them, he is led to question the certainty of his own religious beliefs; therefore he may be weakened in his willingness to persecute those who do not share those beliefs.

Having arbitrarily nominated Christianity the best religion, Buckingham refuses to choose among the various sects of Christian belief. "And here, I must leave every Man to take pains, in seeking out, and chusing for himself; he only being answerable to God Almighty for his own Soul" (18). If each Christian is responsible only to God, no Christian may be forced by other men to alter his beliefs. Here Buckingham reaches the climax and real point of his discourse. He asks a series of rhetorical questions directed at "those ... who are pleas'd to call themselves Christians:

First, Whether there be any thing more directly opposite to the Doctrine and Practice of *Jesus Christ*, than to use any kind of Force upon Men, in Matters of Religion? And consequently, Whether all those that practice it, (Let them be of what *Church*, or *Sect*, they please) ought not justly to be call'd *Anti-christians?*

Further questions suggest that the use of force in religious disputes is not only anti-Christian, but also childish and impolitic. Buckingham concludes with a word of "Friendly Advice" to his Christian readers: "Let them endeavour, by their good Counsel, and good Example, to perswade others to lead such Lives, as may save their Souls: And not be perpetually quarrelling amongst themselves, and cutting one another's Throats" (19–21). None of Buckingham's leading questions or the conclusion drawn from them really depends upon the preceding train of reasoning. Nor has that train of reasoning taken the inevitable direction which Buckingham has claimed for it in his foreword. The questions with which the *Discourse* began were cosmological. They were confusingly stated and so interrupted by digressions that it was nearly impossible to follow them. The questions with which it ends are social, practical, and political. They are clearly stated, easy to understand—and loaded.

If we examine the *Discourse* as a work of kinetic art, asking not what it means, but what it does to its reader as he makes his way through it, we can see that the reader is likely to be distracted and uncertain when he thinks that he is considering fundamenal theological issues, but that he is allowed to think clearly when he is reading of the consequences of persecution and the value of toleration. He may conclude the *Discourse*, therefore, feeling that basic theological issues are vague at best, but that every man ought to be his own guide, and that if we know anything with certainty, it is that religious persecution is wrong. A reader who responds this way, of course, vindicates Buckingham's renunciation of logic as a persuasive tool in matters of religion.

The *Short Discourse* is to Buckingham's nondramatic prose what *The Rehearsal* is to his dramatic works: his most complex and most polished production, operating on more than one level, manipulating its audience and diverting them. But whereas *The Rehearsal* attempts to influence its audience's attitude toward the theater by raising the level of their awareness, the *Short Discourse* attempts to change its readers' minds by deceiving and confusing them.[29] It would be satisfying to be able to report that the *Discourse* had the effect that Buckingham intended. But in fact, the period immediately after its publication was one of sharply increased persecution, largely as a result of the failure of Monmouth's Rebellion, crushed in July 1685, which was seen by High-Church Tories as one more attempt by the Dissenters to seize power. Some measure of religious toleration came later in the reign of King James, when both the king and Parliament found it useful to woo the support of the Dissenters by making concessions to them—but by then the duke was dead.

Buckingham was a member of the circle of talented and noble amateur writers and critics whom we now call the Restoration court wits.[30] If we keep in mind that the court wits generally wrote not to publish, but to amuse themselves and their friends, and the fact that they considered "ease" in writing a stylistic characteristic of the highest value, we can see that Buckingham's work represents both his own mind and the milieu in which it was produced. He has not the genius of a Rochester, but his nondramatic works can be compared with those of any of the other court wits. And throughout his writing, in prose and verse, we see evidence of his intelligence, his talent for mockery, and that energy and imagination which, to both friend and foe, were the identifying characteristics of George Villiers. If today we still find the qualities of his mind appealing, certainly that fact should be no surprise.

Chapter Three
Buckingham's Minor Dramatic Works

Buckingham's fame as a dramatist rests today entirely upon *The Rehearsal*. Few scholars have read any of his other plays, and probably no living person has ever seen a performance of any of them. Yet at least one play among them is good enough to deserve continued interest, and all of them can help us to understand the development of Buckingham's talent leading up to and following his best-known work. The duke's minor dramatic works include two revisions of plays by Beaumont and Fletcher, an intrigue comedy written in collaboration with Sir Robert Howard but never performed, a comic sketch, and an unfinished heroic drama in blank verse.

The Chances

Buckingham's first dramatic work to be performed was his revision of the comedy *The Chances*, written by John Fletcher probably about 1617, an adaptation for the stage of *La Senora Cornelia*, a novella by Cervantes first published in 1613. The subject of the play is the attempted elopement of the duke of Ferrara with a noblewoman named Constantia, the sister of Petruchio, the governor of Bologna. The "chances" of the title are coincidences, which at first frustrate the elopement. At the end of the play, Constantia and the duke are reunited, largely through the efforts of Don John and Don Frederick, two Spanish gentleman students, who shelter Constantia and her infant son in their flight from Petruchio, effect a reconciliation between Petruchio and the duke, and eventually bring all the parties together.

One of the coincidences indicated by the title is the appearance in the play of another character named Constantia, a whore, mistress to Antonio, one of Petruchio's attendants. When Antonio is wounded, this second Constantia steals his gold and flees. At about the same time, the first Constantia leaves Don John's and Don Frederick's lodgings with her infant and Gillian, the two students' landlady. Petruchio, the duke, and the two students, seeking to find the first Constantia, are led by mistake to seize the second. Eventually the men go to the house of Peter Vechio, a supposed conjuror, to ask for information about Constantia and Gillian. Vechio, pretending to raise spirits, presents Constantia to them, and the play ends happily.

Petruchio and the duke are fairly standard heroic characters, the first concerned primarily with his honor, the second with his love. Constantia is charming in her beauty and appealing in her distress. Don Frederick, though somewhat more realistically drawn, is equally heroic. His treatment of Constantia is gracious, courageous, and unselfish. The comic characters in the play are old Antonio, the fierce fighter, whoremaster, and toper; Gillian, the sharp-tongued and somewhat hysterical old landlady; and Don John, the extravagant rake. Except for Don John, the most important characters are too noble to be truly comic.

As written by Fletcher, *The Chances* has one serious defect: the plot runs out of energy after the third act. Although the flight of Constantia and the landlady and the confusion of her with Antonio's whore offered an opportunity for repeated complications, Fletcher did not exploit it. The second Constantia, the whore, appears onstage only briefly, and she and her bawd are stock comic characters. The final scene at the house of Peter Vechio contains little more than spectacle. Since there is no particular reason why Gillian and the first Constantia should have taken shelter there, the scene is less a resolution of the complications of the plot than simply an end to them.

Buckingham's revision of the play, first performed in 1667, supplies an entirely new fourth and fifth act. He lessens the importance of Gillian, the landlady, by depriving her of some of her richest lines, and he alters the character of Antonio. But he creates an entirely new comic character, the mother of the second Constantia, whose presence compensates the audience for whatever it has lost from those two characters. Most importantly, he greatly enriches the character of the second Constantia, turning her from a crude, insolent whore into an appealingly witty, self-possessed woman. In her cheerful, direct libertinism, she is a perfect comic partner to Don John:

> 2 *Constantia.* This sinning without pleasure I cannot endure; to have always a remorse, and ne'er do anything that should cause it, is intolerable.... Well, I'll no more on 't; for to be frighted with Death and Damnation both at once is a little too hard. I do here vow I'll live forever chast, or find out some handsome young fellow I can love; I think that's the better. (4. 1, p. 45)[1]

Buckingham improves the plot of Fletcher's play by means of a fairly simple but very effective device. Instead of having Don John, Don Frederick, the duke, and Petruchio go together to seek the first Constantia and the landlady, he separates them. Now he can have Don John meet the second Constantia when the others have not, and then have the arrival of the others precipitate new misunderstandings. As the first Constantia flees her brother and the second flees from Antonio, each discovery leads to a new flight and new discoveries. But when, in act 5, scene 3, Don Frederick discovers from the mother of the second Constantia that there are two women named Constantia, the resolution of the plot proceeds quickly and naturally to its conclusion.

In addition, Buckingham's new plot devices create a kind of second plot, which runs roughly parallel to the first and serves as an illuminating contrast to it. The idea of contrast, of course, existed in Fletcher's version of the play. The fact that the whore, the most inconstant of women, shares the name *Constantia* with the heroine is obviously a comic irony. (Cervantes's novella also has two women with the same name, but their name is Cornelia, rather than Constantia.) But Buckingham develops the idea much farther. He creates, in the characters of Don John and the second Constantia, two anti-Platonic lovers whose carnal urgency becomes a comic foil to the nobility and unselfishness of the first Constantia and Don Frederick.

For example, in the scene where the first Constantia and Don Frederick meet, Frederick's immediate response to Constantia's appeal shows his susceptibility to the claims of honor:

> *Constantia.* As ever you lov'd honour,
> As ever your desires may gain their ends,
> Do a poor wretched Woman but this Benefit,
> For I am forc't to trust ye.

Frederick. Y' 'ave charm'd me,
Humanity and Honour bids me help ye;
And if I fail your trust ———
Constantia. The time's too dangerous
To stay your protestations. I believe ye,
Alas, I must believe ye....
. . . . . .
Frederick. Come be hearty,
He must strike through my life that takes
You from me. (1. 7, pp. 8–9)

Much later in the play, Don John is in frantic pursuit of the second Constantia when by chance he runs into the first, who seeks his aid. Don John's indifference to her appeal contrasts sharply with Don Frederick's earlier response:

1 Constantia. Hold, Don John, hold.
John. Ha? is it you my Dear?
1 Constantia. For Heaven's sake Sir, carry me from hence, or I'm utterly undone.
John. Phoo pox, this is th' other: now could I almost beat her, for making me the Proposition: Madam, there are some a coming that will do it a great deal better; but I am in such haste, that I vow to Gad Madam—
. . . .
1 Constantia. Good Sir, be not so cruel, as to leave me in this distress.
John. No, no, no; I'm only going a little way, and will be back presently.
1 Constantia. But pray Sir hear me; I'm in that danger—
John. No, no, no, I vow to Gad Madam, no danger i' the World, let me alone, I warrant you. (5. 2, pp. 54–55)

Don Frederick, acting as a man of honor, treats Constantia with respect and consideration, though he has never met her before. Don John, driven by what he thinks of as love, neglects the duty that humanity and honor set before him. In the second scene, the first Constantia and Don John seem almost to be characters from two different worlds. We have something of the same feeling we have in watching Stoppard's *Rosencrantz and Guildenstern Are Dead*: that a person from our own world has somehow wandered into the sublime world of tragedy, where every word, action or gesture is invested with superhuman significance. But whereas Stoppard's Rosencrantz and Guildenstern can neither understand nor control what happens to them in the world of *Hamlet*, in this play the world is Don John's and it is the heroic characters who have wandered into it. It is their blunders, after all, which keep frustrating his efforts to arrange a tryst with the second Constantia. And in the scene above, it is the first Constantia who is helpless; to Don John at this point she is merely a nuisance.

A similar contrast occurs in two revelation scenes, one chaste, the other sexual. After rescuing the first Constantia, Don Frederick asks that she draw aside her veil and reveal herself to him:

> *Frederick.* Draw but that Cloud aside, to satisfie me
> For what good Angel I am engag'd.
> *Constantia.* It shall be.
> For I am truly confident ye are honest:
> The piece is scarce worth looking on.
> *Frederick.* Trust me,
> The abstract of all beauty, soul of sweetness,
> Defend me honest thoughts, I shall grow wild else.
> What eyes are there, rather what little Heavens,
> To stir mens contemplations? what a Paradise
> Runs through each part she has? Good Blood be temperate:
> I must look off: too excellent an object
> Confounds the Sense that sees it.

In a corresponding scene, the face of the second Constantia inspires quite different thoughts in Don John:

> *John.* Come, pray unmasque.
> *2 Constantia.* Then turn away your face; for I'm resolved you shall not see a bit of mine till I have set it in order, and then—
> *John.* What?
> *2 Constantia.* I'll strike you dead.
> *John.* A mettled Whore, I warrant her; come if she be now but young, and have but a nose on her face, she'll

	be as good as her word: I'm e'en panting for breath already.
2 Constantia.	Now stand your ground if you dare.
John.	By this light a rare creature! ten thousand times handsomer than her we seek for! this can be sure no common one: pray Heaven she be a Whore. (4. 2, p. 47)

The first Constantia's beauty is evidence of her pure soul. Don Frederick, recognizing that fact, calls her a "good Angel" and uses the words "Heavens" and "Paradise" to describe her. He sees her as so excellent a sight, both physically and morally, that she confounds his senses. Don John's senses, on the other hand, far from being confounded, are stimulated to the last degree. The second Constantia, rather than seeing herself as "scarce worth looking on," is confident that with the help of her makeup she can "strike [Don John] dead." Whereas the first Constantia and Don Frederick are drawn together by the sublime nobility of both their souls, the second Constantia sees that she will have to rely upon her beauty and her arts to gain Don John's favor. And just as Heaven has sent Don Frederick to the aid of the first Constantia in her distress, so both members of the second couple see in one another the answer to their prayers: she recognizes in Don John the "handsome young fellow" she has been seeking, and Don John's prayer to heaven that the second Constantia be a whore will be answered. In each of the pairs of scenes we have just examined, the first was written by Fletcher and retained in Buckingham's version of the play, the second added by Buckingham. In this heightened contrast between the nobility of Don Frederick and the first Constantia on the one hand and the frank sexuality of Don John and the second Constantia on the other lies Buckingham's chief contribution to the meaning of the play.

The scenes between Don John and the second Constantia provide opportunities for bawdy wit:

2 Constantia.	Hark ye Sir, I ought now to use you very scurvily, but I can't find it in my heart to do it.
John.	Then God's blessing on thy heart for it.
2 Constantia.	But a—
John.	What?
2 Constantia.	I would fain—
John.	I, so would I: come let's go.

2 Constantia.	I would fain know whether you can be kind to me.
John.	That thou shalt presently; come away.
2 Constantia.	And will you always?
John.	Always? I can't say so; but I will as often as I can.
2 Constantia.	Phoo! I mean love me.
John.	Well, I mean that too. (5. 4, p. 59)

The urgency of Don John's sexual desires is highly comic, and the double meaning of the phrases used by both lovers parodies the vows of the conventional lovers in heroic drama. But Don John's statement to the second Constantia that he means to "love" her as often as he can is more than merely double entendre; it tells us something important about his way of thinking. Apparently, to him the word "love" means simply sex. When he next sees the first Constantia, he apologizes to her for his earlier neglect in these words:

John.	I was before distracted, and 'tis not strange the love of her should hinder me from remembering what was due to you, since it made me forget my self.
1 Constantia.	Sir, I do know too well the power of Love, by my own experience, not to pardon all the effects of it in another. (5. 4, p. 60)

When the first Constantia speaks of the power of love, she speaks heroically, of the force which has led her to alienate her family, risk her life, and bear a child out of wedlock, all for love of the duke. By comparison, Don John's use of the word is comically trivial. Thus the contrast in this exchange suggests the limitations of Don John's view of life and love. He may move easily through the world, but he moves lightly, too, skimming along its surface and knowing nothing of its depths. He cannot experience life as profoundly as someone like the first Constantia.

In the character of the mother of the second Constantia, Buckingham created a highly amusing character, a pretentious, affected, and self-deceived hypocrite who, though she has sold her daughter to Antonio and has later stolen more gold from him, insists that she guides herself by the highest principles of honor:

2 Constantia.	Dear Mother, let us go a little faster to secure ourselves from Antonio; for my part I am in that terrible

	fright, that I can neither think, speak, nor stand still, till we are safe a Shipboard, and out of sight of the Shore.
Mother.	Out of sight o' the Shore? why, do ye think I'll depatriate?
2 Constantia.	Depatriate? what's that?
Mother.	Why, ye Fool you, leave my Country: what will you never learn to speak out of the vulgar road?
2 Constantia.	O Lord, this hard word will undo us.
Mother.	As I'm a Christian, if it were to save my honour (which is ten thousand times dearer to me than my life) I would not be guilty of so odious a thought.
2 Constantia.	Pray Mother, since your honour is so dear to ye, consider that if we are taken, both it and we are lost for ever.
Mother.	Ay Girle, but what will the world say, if they should hear so odious a thing of us, as that we should depatriate? (4. 1, pp. 44–45)

Buckingham invested the mother of the second Constantia with two qualities which always make a comic character memorable on the stage: she has a predominant passion (in this case, for social climbing) and a style of speaking (in this case her inappropriately elevated diction) which makes that passion instantly recognizable.

Although his most important changes are in the fourth and fifth acts of the play, which he completely rewrote, Buckingham made a number of smaller changes in the first three acts in order to eliminate some small inconsistencies and to prepare for his later changes. For example, he changed the scene of the play from Bologna to Naples, because the second Constantia and her accomplice are said in act 4, scene 2 (act 3, scene 5 of Buckingham's version) to have fled "to the port." Bologna is an inland city, so Naples fits the line better. Since Naples is not a university town, he changed Don John and Don Frederick from students to young gentlemen on their travels. In act 3, scene 5 (scene 4 in Buckingham's version), Fletcher had Don John and Don Frederick overhear a soliloquy by Francisco, in which Francisco mentions the flight of the second Constantia; it is this episode which leads each of the two young men to suspect the other of concealing the first Constantia. But one of the conventions of Renaissance and Jacobean drama is that a soliloquy represents the thoughts of a character and is unheard by the other characters on the stage. Therefore Buckingham added another character ("a Man") and turned the soliloquy into a dialogue, which Don John and Don Frederick could overhear with dramatic propriety.

At several points throughout the first three acts, Buckingham cut lines of exposition which tended to delay the action of the play. The scene in which Antonio is treated by his surgeon (3. 2), for example, was cut to about half the length it had in Fletcher, necessarily omitting some good comic lines, but speeding the action. Since Buckingham wished to make Antonio impotent and to make his impotence crucial to the resolution of the plot (see the exchange between him and the second Constantia [5. 4, p. 60] and her lament [4. 1, p. 45]), he changed Antonio's line, "Will it please you sir / To let me have a wench?" (3.2, 17–18) in Fletcher's play to "Will't please you, Sir, to give me a brimmer?" (35).[2]

The most important changes Buckingham made in the first three acts were those which served to differentiate more fully the characters of Don John and Don Frederick and to make them more consistent. For example, in order to make the two Constantias more distinct, Buckingham got rid of some suggestions of erotic attraction between Don John and the first Constantia; thus in the scene in which they first meet, when Don John says to the first Constantia, "Nay, 'tis certaine, / Thou art the sweetest woman I e'er looked on: / I hope thou art not honest" (2.3, 20–22), Buckingham cut "I hope thou art not honest." Later in the same scene, at the urging of Frederick, Don John kisses Constantia in greeting, then remarks out of earshot of the other two,

> Now 'tis impossible I should be honest;
> She kisses with a conjuration
> Would make the devill dance: what points she at?
> My leg I warrant, or my well knit body:
> Sit fast Don Frederick. (2.3, 58–62)

Buckingham cut "She kisses with a conjuration / Would make the devill dance." These changes eliminate the faint possibility that the chaste first Constantia might attract, deliberately or otherwise, Don John's sexual attentions. In fact, in Buckingham's version of the play she is the only woman to whom he is sexually indifferent; even Gillian, the aged landlady, is the object of a few passing leers. These changes are important because Buckingham wished to make the two Constantias touchstones for the contrasting characters of the two young men. For a related reason, he cut one of the few scenes whose loss in any way harms the play. In act 3, scene 1, Don John teases Gillian, the landlady, mercilessly with sexual, sometimes obscene, taunts:

> Worshipful Lady,
> How does thy Velvet Scabbard? by this hand
> Thou lookest most amiably: now could I willingly
> (And 'twere not for abusing thy Geneva print there,)
> Venture my Body with thee. (3.1, 74–78)

In Fletcher's play, Gillian finally replies, predicting that John will sing another tune after his whoring has gained him a few venereal diseases. Her mockery of Don John is satisfying and poetically just, and its absence from Buckingham's play is a real loss of comedy, but for his purposes it was unsuitable to her character. Since he intended her to stand in something of the same relationship to the first Constantia as the mother does to the second (that is, as protector and advisor), it was important that no bawdy pass her lips.

Almost all readers and critics have acknowledged that Buckingham's changes in *The Chances* improved the play. Dryden wrote in 1672, "Fletcher's Don John is our only bugbear; and yet I may affirm, without suspicion of flattery, that he now speaks better, and that his character is maintained with much more vigour in the fourth and fifth acts than it was by Fletcher in the three former. I have always acknowledged the wit of our predecesors, with all the veneration which becomes me; but, I am sure, their wit was not that of gentlemen; there was ever somewhat that was ill-bred and clownish in it, and which confessed the conversation of the authors."[3] It is not easy to see how Dryden might have thought that Buckingham had made Don John less ill-bred; the duke retained most of his obscene and double entendre speeches from Fletcher's play and even added to them. But certainly Dryden is correct that the character of Don John, which is the mainspring of the play, has more vigor in the two final acts as Buckingham has revised them. A. C. Sprague, with the perspective of two hundred fifty years, has written, "In short, Fletcher's comedy has been genuinely improved by its Restoration adapter—a somewhat extraordinary thing in itself. And the improvement has been gained by entering fully into the spirit of the original and applying a simple technical device by which that spirit might be maintained at its best."[4]

Buckingham's adaptation of *The Chances* is one of his most successful works, and it was an immediate hit. Displacing Fletcher's original from the stage, it was performed regularly throughout the Restoration and well into the second half of the eighteenth century. It is no wonder that the success of this play encouraged the duke to try his hand again at writing for the stage.

The Country Gentleman

For more than three hundred years, the play *The Country Gentleman* was known only in the story of the political controversy it provoked, for the play itself had been suppressed. In 1976 the full text of the play was published by Arthur H. Scouten and Robert D. Hume, who found a manuscript copy of it in the Folger Shakespeare Library in Washington.[5]

The play, which was scheduled for performance on 27 February 1669, was suppressed because it became the occasion for a crisis which rocked the government of England. The cause of the crisis was the fact that the play included two characters which were clearly recognizable caricatures of Sir William Coventry and Sir John Duncomb, Coventry's friend and ally on the Privy Council. Both men were supporters of the duke of York, King Charles's brother and heir apparent to the throne, whom Buckingham always opposed when he could. The two characters, Sir Cautious Trouble-all and Sir Gravity Empty, are portrayed in several scenes as grave, foolish, self-important "men of business"; Empty, a sycophant, simply repeats the thoughts of Trouble-all in slightly different words:

> *Cautious.* For counsell you shall not want it, and in the first place have a care of your Landlady.
> *Lucy.* Why Sir?
> *Empty.* Why the reason is plain, I say as Sir Cautious said, have a care of your Landlady by all means.
> *Cautious.* Ladies she is a woman of contrivances.
> *Empty.* That is of tricks.
> *Kate.* A most admirable explanation.

> Cautious. And of small credit with her neighbors.
> Empty. Of little or none at all. (2.1. 176–85)

What made the identification of Sir Cautious Trouble-all with Sir William Coventry unmistakable was the inclusion in the play of a scene in which Sir Cautious explains to Sir Gravity his use of a round table with a round hole in its middle, in which he can sit on a swivel-stool and turn himself. His idea is to arrange his papers on the table in a circle about him, according to their topics, and then to turn himself from one to another as he moves from one topic to another. As members of the Privy Council all knew, Sir William had invented just such a table, which he used in his study at home, and he had very proudly displayed it to curious visitors. (Samuel Pepys, for example, had seen the table on 4 July 1668.)[6]

As Coventry himself told the story to Pepys, when he heard of the plan to present the play, "he told Tom. Killigrew [the manager of the Theatre Royal, where the play was to be presented] that he should tell his actors, whoever they were, that did offer at anything like representing him, that he would not complain to my Lord Chamberlain, which was too weak, nor get him beaten, as Sir. Ch. Sidly is said to do, but that he would cause his nose to be cut."[7] And he sent his nephew, Henry Saville, to carry to Buckingham a challenge to a duel.

Although Buckingham was an excellent swordsman and Coventry was not, the duke did not want to fight the duel. It had been only a little more than a year since the infamous duel at Barn Elms, when Buckingham had killed the earl of Shrewsbury. If he were now to kill Coventry, especially after having provoked the quarrel, the scandal might destroy his political career. Fortunately for him, the duel could easily be prevented. He had only to allow word of it to leak out before it could take place, and it would be officially stopped. According to Pepys, King Charles asked both men at a meeting of the Privy Council whether it was true that Coventry had sent a challenge to Buckingham. Buckingham admitted that he had received it. Coventry declined to answer, but the king took his silence as an admission of guilt, and he issued a warrant for the commitment of Coventry to the Tower of London.[8] The king's lawyers had found an old law, from the time of King Henry VII, which made it a felony to conspire the death of a member of the king's Privy Council. Since Buckingham (like Coventry himself) was a privy counsellor, the law applied in this case. Coventry was dismissed from all his official positions, though he was released from the Tower and pardoned on 21 March and the play was forbidden to be performed or published.

By means of this maneuver, Buckingham had scored an important victory. He had deprived his enemy, the duke of York, of an able and highly placed ally. He had driven a wedge between York and the king. And in addition, he had pleased the king, who wrote of Coventry to his sister, "The truth of it is, he has been a troublesome man...., and I am well rid of him."[9]

Because at least one contemporary report said that Buckingham had "inserted a scene" into a play already written by Howard, Scouten and Hume have thought it most likely that only the "oyster-table scene" was the work of Buckingham.[10] But the precise extent of any collaboration is difficult for outsiders—even when they are contemporaries—to ascertain. There is some internal evidence that Buckingham may have had a hand in the fabric of the entire play.

The most interesting piece of such evidence is the resemblance between the character of Mistress Finical Fart, the affected, scheming landlady in *The Country Gentleman*, and that of the mother of the second Constantia in Buckingham's revision of *The Chances*, which had been performed for the first time only two years earlier. Both Mistress Finical and the mother are loquacious, both imagine themselves to be well-bred, and both affect French diction. There is a striking similarity, for example, between this complaint by Mrs. Finical: "I cannot express myself with a *bonne mine*, but they fall upon me with a most unbred audaciousness" (*Country Gentleman*, 1. 1. 37–40)—and this remark by the mother of the second Constantia: "Besides, with all her wit, Constantia is but a Fool, and calls all the Meniarderies of a bonne mine, affectation" (*Chances*, 5. 3, p. 56).[11] Although Frenchified fops are standard figures of fun on the Restoration stage (see, for example, Sir Fopling Flutter in Etherege's *The Man of Mode* and Melantha in Dryden's *Marriage à la Mode*), such characters are usually upper-class figures. Indeed, Hume and Scouten, apparently forgetting about the mother in *The Chances*, call Mrs. Finical "a figure almost without parallel in seventeenth century comedy."[12] For Howard to have borrowed the use of this figure from Buckingham's play would have been a most uncharacteristic act, but for Buckingham to use the same kind of character twice, particularly when the first had met with success, would be natural.

Another parallel with *The Chances*, though a slighter one, occurs in act 1, scene 1, where Worthy, arriving somewhat drunk at Mrs.

Finical's house, calls her "my belov'd" and pretends to make her a sexual proposition. Presumably he is only teasing her, for she is past middle age and no beauty, and he is one of the young wits who are the heroes of the play. The scene has a parallel in *The Chances*, act 3, scene 1, where Don John teases Gillian, his landlady, in much the same way. The scene in *The Chances* was written by Fletcher, not by Buckingham, but Buckingham had retained it, with modifications, when he revised the play, and it would have been fresh in his mind in 1669 if he had wished to draw upon it for *The Country Gentleman*.

The dialogue between Sir Cautious and Sir Gravity quoted above (2. 1. 172–200) is very much like one which appeared in 1671 in *The Rehearsal*, act 2, scene 4, in which the two politicians, the Physician and the Gentleman-Usher, "lay their heads together" to discuss the knotty point of whether the two kings of Brentford overheard their whisper (pp. 22–23 in the Crane edition). Indeed, some unknown annotator has written in a contemporary hand in a 1683 folio copy of *The Rehearsal*, "Sr Wm Couentry Sr John Duncomb."[13] Of course, Buckingham might well have copied the scene from *The Country Gentleman* even if Howard had written it. But taken together, these three similarities between *The Country Gentleman* and other works of Buckingham's are persuasive, though not conclusive, evidence that the duke collaborated with Howard in the composition of the whole play.

The plot of *The Country Gentleman* involves Isabella and Philadelphia, the two daughters of Sir Richard Plainbred, the country gentleman of the title, and their three pairs of suitors. The suitors are Worthy and Lovetruth, two young men who, like the girls and their father, are from the country but are living temporarily in London; Vapor and Slander, two London fops, elaborate in their dress and speech but completely without honor; and Sir Cautious Trouble-all and Sir Gravity Empty, the self-important, grave "men of business" already mentioned. The fops and the politicians are interested not in the young ladies' persons (which when the play begins they have not seen), but in their fortunes, of which they have heard enough. Mistress Finical plots to support the interest of Vapor and Slander, for she is impressed by their foppish manner. Trim, a clever barber and former servant of Sir Richard's, pretends to be supporting the interest of Sir Cautious and Sir Gravity, but in fact he hopes to arrange a marriage between them and his own daughters, Lucy and Kate, as a means of making his own fortune. In the end, as a result of several complicated schemes, Trim succeeds in marrying the politicians to his daughters, and Isabella and Philadelphia are married to Worthy and Lovetruth, respectively. Vapor and Slander are "married" to two footboys, servants to Sir Richard, who have appeared in disguise at the ceremony, and whom the fops have been led to believe are the two heiresses.

The Country Gentleman is an amusing, though not an outstanding, comedy. Like many Restoration comedies, it has an intrigue plot and witty "love duels" between the male and female leads. But neither the witty banter nor the intrigues are dramatically important elements. Because the fops and the politicians pose no serious threat to the heroes' prospects with the heroines, all the plotting of Mrs. Finical is in vain. And whereas the love debates in the "gay couple" tradition derive their spirit from the participants' feeling themselves impelled by love toward marriage and their struggling against the loss of freedom which marriage implies,[14] in *The Country Gentleman* we have no real sense that either the women or the men are really reluctant to marry. The ladies tease the gentlemen, but except when they pretend to believe the fops' account of the abortive duel (4. 1, p. 127) and when they pretend to back out at the last minute before the marriage (5. 1, pp. 145–46), the men know they are being teased, and they relish the interplay as much as the ladies. The audience can enjoy the comic action without ever having to worry about the outcome of the plot.

In several important respects *The Country Gentleman* is atypical of the comedies of its time. One of the chief of these is that all the sensible characters despise the environment and values of London. They denounce urban fashions as nonsense, urban amusements as trivial and useless, and urban dealing as duplicity. Sir Richard, who is in London to transact legal business, hates the city and hopes to return to his home in the West Country as soon as possible. And whereas in most Restoration comedies a country squire who hated the city and longed for the days of Queen Elizabeth would be a fool, in this play Sir Richard's sentiments are echoed by his beautiful and clever daughters and by their witty suitors, Worthy and Lovetruth. Only the fools, led by Mrs. Finical, love the city.

Of the principal characters' objections to the city, the one which carries the most weight is the idea that it is a place of deception. Thus Trim says of Sir Richard, "He swears he lives here in ignorance, and the plainest dealing he us'd to find was among the Lyons, for he knew when they were angry by their roaring; he never understood what fine people meant, either by what they said or did" (52). And Lovetruth, when he hears Vapor and Slander attempting to court the pretended heiresses by boasting of their supposed attractiveness and courage, says in an aside, "How I kindle at these lyes—" (104). Fancy speeches are invariably undercut, even when the intelligent characters make them. For example, when Worthy and Lovetruth first approach the heroines, Worthy begins with a conventional compliment, "Save you Ladies, this [that is, the pleasure of their company] is a happiness above our merits." Isabella replies, "Why truly if you speak as you think, you deserve very little" (84). In another scene, all four lovers mock the conventional Petrarchan formulas:

Worthy. And shall we part thus?
Lovetruth. But one kind word.
Worthy. Or a speaking look.
Isabella. Nay, if you are so reasonable, have at you, come Sister, lets give 'em looks apeece. (*They look at 'em.*)
Worthy. Umh, so it goes through and through; Lovetruth, prithee look behind me and see where the look comes out.
Lovetruth. No man, tis but got to thy heart yet— (3.1, p. 113)

In scenes of banter like these, Worthy and Lovetruth show that they deserve the love of the two witty ladies, in part because they do not expect them to believe the common cant.

However, since the play assigns a high value to truth and plain-dealing, it is hard for an audience to accept the fact that all the supposedly moral characters in the play—Worthy, Lovetruth, Isabella, Philadelphia, Kate, and Lucy—participate in deceptions of their own, designed to trick the fools. Sir Richard, who never takes an active part in the action but is always told of it afterward, invariably applauds these deceptions. Tricky plots are the stuff of which comedies are made, but to have all the heroes and heroines of the play engage in behavior which violates the play's highest values is confusing or worse.

Another problem concerns the fact that the play's action takes place in a single setting, Mrs. Finical's boardinghouse, and within a single day. This observance of the classical "unities" (which, interestingly enough, Howard had attacked as a critical dogma a year or two before),[15] gives the play a tight structure, but it puts a strain on credibility. An audience can hardly believe that two intelligent young ladies like Isabella and Philadelphia would be willing to marry on the same day they have come to London and have met their suitors, particularly in the light of their dryly amused manner toward the young men. To partly overset that objection, Howard and Buckingham plant the idea that Worthy and Lovetruth have known the two girls before. Lovetruth tells Worthy after the scene of meeting, "To see the luck on't, that our first loves should be brought after us, tis a good omen," and Isabella and Philadelphia acknowledge having received some attentions from the men at their father's house in the country (84). Still, the action happens too fast. Even though Sir Cautious and Sir Gravity are too stupid to pay attention to the girls' reactions and Vapor and Slander are too blinded by greed, it is hard to believe that they could be led to expect the girls to marry them on the day they have just met.

Another critical problem is raised by the authors' use of characters in pairs. Both Buckingham and Howard had previously used this device, a common formula on the Restoration comic stage.[16] In this play the formula is carried to an extreme, for there are two heiresses, Isabella and Philadelphia; two barbers' daughters, Kate and Lucy; two wits, Worthy and Lovetruth; two fops, Vapor and Slander; two men of business, Sir Cautious and Sir Gravity; two plotters, Trim and Mrs. Finical; and even two footboys, Ned and Will. The only character who does not appear as part of a pair is Sir Richard Plainbred, the Country Gentleman, and his appearing alone certainly makes him stand out in the play, as does his not participating in the intrigues of the plot. But that singularity is not exploited.

The fact that all the major characters except Sir Richard are doubled makes possible some of the intrigues involved in the plots: for example, the marriage trick could not be played on Vapor and Slander without the participation of one sister in the fooling of each. However, the doubled characters are, in most cases, insufficiently differentiated. We have no trouble telling Trim from Mrs. Finical, of course, and Sir Cautious can be distinguished from his echo, Sir Gravity, if only by his always speaking any given idea first. But the members of the other pairs are nearly indistinguishable. Isabella and Philadelphia are both witty and independent; Vapor and Slander are both foolish and underhanded. The lines assigned to either member of any pair might as easily be given to the other. Thus, many scenes, not only those of the fools, but even those of the intelligent characters, become a kind of litany in which one character finishes the thoughts of another. This problem probably shows the effect of Howard's hand, for Buckingham's treatment of Don John and Don Frederick, in his revision of *The Chances*, suggests that he preferred to emphasize the differences between paired characters.

For all these reasons, *The Country Gentleman* is a flawed play. Both Buckingham and Howard had written better comedies before this one, and Buckingham was to write a much better one later in *The Rehearsal*. Ironically, the king's suppression of this play prevented the public from knowing of a comedy that would have diminished its authors' reputations.

The Restauration: or, Right Will Take Place

Buckingham's *The Restauration* is a revision of *Philaster: Or, Love Lies a-Bleeding*, written by Beaumont and Fletcher in 1610. Although the evidence that Buckingham was the author of the revision is inconclusive, it has been persuasive enough to convince most authoritative scholars and editors.[17]

The plot of Beaumont's and Fletcher's tragicomedy focuses on Philaster, son of the late king of Sicily, and his beloved, Arathusa, the daughter of the king of Calabria. Because Arathusa's father has usurped the Sicilian throne from Philaster's father, the couple must communicate in secret; therefore Philaster orders his page, Bellario, to enter the service of the princess.

The king plans a marriage between Arathusa and Pharamond, a Spanish prince. To defeat the plan, Arathusa informs her father of an assignation between Pharamond and Megra, a lascivious court lady. The king, outraged, orders both Pharamond and Megra to leave Sicily, but Megra, to mitigate her guilt, accuses Arathusa of a sexual involvement with Bellario. For some reason the king and his court believe the accusation. Dion, a respected Sicilian lord, passes the story on to Philaster, saying that he himself caught the pair in the act.

Philaster parts angrily with both his mistress and his page and flees to the forest to be alone. Arathusa and Bellario, separately, take to the forest, too. Eventually Arathusa faints, Bellario happens upon her and attempts to aid her, and Philaster, coming upon the two together, wounds Arathusa. Eventually he wounds Bellario, too, but both the lady and the boy remain loyal to him.

When Philaster is captured and held for execution by the king on the charge of attacking the princess, Arathusa arranges to have Philaster placed in her custody, and they are secretly married. The townspeople, hearing that Philaster is under sentence of death, rise up in rebellion and seize Pharamond. The king promises to release Philaster and recognize his marriage to Arathusa if he will quell the uprising. He does so, order is restored, and Bellario reveals that "he" is really a woman, Euphrasia, daughter of Dion, who has secretly loved Philaster and has disguised herself as a boy in order to serve him.

Buckingham's revisions of the play were prompted by a consciousness that the earlier version lacked what Restoration audiences considered "refinement." Buckingham's contemporaries were troubled when in Renaissance dramas, including this one, lords and ladies sometimes exchanged bawdy jokes. Still more troublesome was the fact that the heroic characters did not always behave heroically. Dryden, for example, in his *Defense of the Epilogue* (1672), had complained that "Philaster wound[s] his mistress, and afterwards his boy, to save himself."[18] As we know from having examined Buckingham's revisions of *The Chances*, the duke felt it important to separate the comic plot and characters from the heroic ones as clearly as possible.

To correct these faults, Buckingham made his most important changes in the fourth act, which takes place in the forest. Whereas Beaumont and Fletcher had Philaster wound Arathusa deliberately and in cold blood, as an act of justice, Buckingham changed the action so that Philander (the counterpart of Philaster in his version) attacks Endymion (Bellario) and wounds Araminta (Arathusa) accidentally.[19] Philaster wounds Bellario while the latter is asleep, but in *The Restauration* Philander wounds Endymion only after Endymion rejects his repeated entreaties to leave him. Both these changes help to rescue the hero of the piece from the imputations of cowardice and cruelty.

Several of Buckingham's changes were intended to produce a sharper separation between the characters. Pharamond in the original play is already somewhat pompous and conceited; in Buckingham's version he (now named "Thrasamond") is a complete fool, unable to speak in public without his governor's prompting. Araminta in Buckingham's version lacks some of the vigor of Arathusa in Beaumont's and Fletcher's; Buckingham cut out the section of her initial interview with Philaster in which she tells him imperiously that she will not relinquish her claim to the two kingdoms of Calabria and Sicily. Buckingham seems to have tried to make her more like Shakespeare's Desdemona, in order to make Philander's wounding her in act 4 more evocative of pity.

Although Buckingham had a gift for comedy, he seems to have believed, as did many of his contemporaries, that the comic and heroic modes could not coexist in a single character or scene. In his revision of *Philaster* he repeatedly cut scenes and lines in which the noble characters engage in humor, particularly if the humor has an obscene cast. For example, he removed scene 1 of act 4, in which the courtiers, preparing for the hunt, laugh and joke about the rumors about Arathusa and about Megra's having been caught the previous evening in Pharamond's chambers. He also removed, perhaps for the same reason, scene 2 of act 2, in which Pharamond and Megra, overheard by Gallatea, arrange their assignation. That cut does particularly serious damage to the play, however, because it removes emphasis from one of the most important complications of the plot. When, in *The Restauration*, Thrasamond is found in Alga's (i.e., Megra's) bedchamber, she seems almost a completely new character, and her accusation against Araminta seems without motive.

In addition to the changes of plot and structure already indicated, Buckingham made small changes in the lines everywhere in the play. Many of these changes are so apparently profitless as to seem meddlesome, and when the scene is in verse, Buckingham's revisions are particularly unfortunate. For example, in act 1, scene 1 of Beaumont's and Fletcher's version of the play, when Philaster first confronts Pharamond, he speaks as follows:

> *Philaster.* Then thus I turne
> My language to you Prince, you forraign man:
> Ne'er stare, nor put on wonder, for you must
> Indure me, and you shall.[20]

In Buckingham's version the same speech begins as follows:

> *Philander.* Thus then—
> I turn myself to you, big foreign man,
> Ne'er stare, nor put on wonder, for you must
> Endure me, and you shall.[21]

The speech in Beaumont and Fletcher is not very good. But in Buckingham's version it is unintentionally comic; the phrase "big foreign man" makes Philander sound like a child. What could Buckingham have hoped to gain by changing "I turne / My language to you" to "I turn myself to you"? The latter represents a slight loss of precision and no apparent gain.

When Arathusa reveals to Philaster that she loves him in Beaumont's and Fletcher's play (1. 2), he replies,

> Madam, you are too full of noble thoughts,
> To lay a traine for this contemned life,
> Which you may have for asking: to suspect
> Were base, where I deserve no ill; love you,
> By all my hopes I doe, above my life....

Buckingham makes Philander more reluctant to believe that Araminta loves him, more hesitant to trust her:

> Oh heavens!
> What is't she means! it cannot sure be love;
> And yet she is too full of noble thoughts
> To lay a train for this contemned life,
> Which she might have for asking: Madam, you
> Perplex my mind so much with what you say,
> I know not what to think....

By making some of Philander's remarks an aside, Buckingham invests him with greater modesty, but he also slows the movement of the play. "I know not what to think," like "big foreign man," seems composed by a writer almost deaf to the decorum of heroic drama—and yet it was certainly composed in an effort to suit the style of the play to that decorum.

When Buckingham began the revision of *Philaster*, he may have had in mind a plan to enrich it with references to the current political scene. His changing its title to *The Restauration* was, of course, one such reference. The epilogue spoken by the Governor, with its references to plots and to Shaftesbury's death, is another. The prologue archly criticizes Buckingham himself for having put his public trust above personal profit when he held his Privy Council posts:

> He, for the publick, needs would play a game,
> For which he has been trounc'd by publick fame;
> And to speak truth, so he deserv'd to be

> For his dull clownish singularity:
> For when the fashion is to break one's trust,
> 'Tis rudeness then to offer to be just.
> (ll. 21-26)

And in the first scene Buckingham added the following exchange:

> *Agremont.* Who is this Prince's father?
> *Cleon.* A person of mean extraction, but by wiles and arts obtaining power, usurp'd the kingdom where he reigns, and keeps it under by a standing army, which our King intends to copy.

The English public had, ever since the Restoration, regarded a standing army in peacetime as an instrument of tyranny. It was deliberately kept to a few small regiments, except in time of war, and in November of 1673 the Parliament had resolved that a standing army was a grievance against the crown.[22]

All these political references are typical of Buckingham's practice, as we have seen in our discussion of *The Country Gentleman* and will see in *The Rehearsal*. But as in those other cases, Buckingham did not develop his innuendoes into a full-fledged satire. Where an opportunity to make a political reference presented itself, he took it, but he did not go to the trouble of seeking such opporunities.

The Restauration has never been performed, and in all probability it never will be. The original play by Beaumont and Fletcher was undistinguished, and Buckingham's revisions, though they removed some of the most objectionable elements in the original, add enough of their own to make it worse. By heightening the distinction between the heroic and the comic, Buckingham succeeded only in making some parts of the play overblown and others trivial. Of all his dramatic works, *The Restauration* is the least successful.

The Battle of Sedgmoor Rehearsed at Whitehall: A Farce

The Battle of Sedgmoor Rehearsed is a short farce written to satirize Louis de Duras, earl of Feversham. Feversham, a loyal adherent of King James since the latter was duke of York, had been born in France and was the nephew of the famous Marshal Turenne, the greatest of Louis XIV's generals. When the duke of Monmouth led his rebellion against King James in June of 1685, Feversham was assigned the command of the royal forces sent to the west of England to defend against the attack.

The Battle of Sedgmoor, in which the royal army destroyed the rebel force, was fought on the night of 5–6 July 1685. After a campaign of several days, in which the two armies had not made significant contact, Feversham encamped on Sedgmoor, outside of Weston Zoyland, a small town a few miles from Bridgewater. There he separated his forces, leaving the foot soldiers in tents on the ground, while he, his officers, and his cavalry were quartered in the village of Weston. The foot, under the command of Colonel John Churchill (the future duke of Marlborough), were protected from an attack over the moor only by a dry ditch, called the Bussex Rine.

Monmouth, who had good intelligence of the size of Feversham's army and its disposition, attempted a surprise attack at night across the moor. Aided by a knowledgeable guide, he managed to slip his army of five thousand men, both infantry and cavalry, across the moor in silence, so that they arrived at the ditch without disclosing their movements. However, at the Rine, the cavalry, under the command of Monmouth's friend Lord Grey, failed to find the plungeon, or ford, and in the confusion the advantage of surprise was lost. Churchill, certainly the greatest military genius of his time, deployed his forces rapidly. Feversham's cannon, which had been guarding the Bridgewater road, were brought up to overlook the ditch, where they raked the rebel troops. Monmouth's army, cut to pieces, never succeeded in crossing the ditch.

As a Frenchman, suspected of Roman Catholicism, and an adherent of King James, Feversham represented to Buckingham all the elements which, in his view, had been brought to power by James's accession to the throne. The fact that King James had used his royal favor to promote an incompetent general must have seemed inevitable to Buckingham, who always regarded James as a stupid man.[23] But Buckingham was not alone in his contempt for Feversham. In January of 1680, the House of Commons had petitioned King Charles II "to remove Lewis, Earl of Feversham, from all military offices and commands, as a promoter of Popery and of the Popish interests."[24] In "A Poem on the Deponents" (1688), an anonymous poet wrote,

> Then in comes Feversham, that haughty beau,
> And tells a tale of "den" and "dat" and "how,"
> Though he's no more believ'd than all the rest;
> Only, poor man, he fain would do his best
> And be rewarded, as when come from th' West.[25]

Buckingham's farce was obviously written soon after the events which it describes, for it mentions details of the battle which audiences might soon forget. Buckingham charges Feversham with having encamped his forces in an indefensible position:

> *Lord.* I suppose, my Lord, that your Lordship was posted in a very strong place.
> *General.* O' begarra, very strong, vid de great river between me and de rebella, calla, de Brooka de Gutter.
> *Lady.* But they say, my Lord, there was no water in that brook of the gutter.
> *General.* Begar, Madama, but dat no be my faulta; begar me no hander de water from coma; if no will rain, begar me no can make de rain.[26]

He points out that the cavalry was separated from the foot soldiers, and that Feversham, as a French nobleman, regarded the common soldiers as rabble:

> *Lady.* But pray, my Lord, why did you not stay with the foot?
> *General.* Begarra, Madama, because dere be great differentia between de gentlemen-officera, and de rogua de sogiera; begarra, de rogua de sogiera lye upon de grounda; but begar, de gentleman-officer go to bedda.

Finally, he makes Feversham in every way an uncomprehending fool:

> *General.* But, my lore, begar me tella you one historia, will make you laffa: Begar de nit o' de battalla me be in bed vid one very pretty womans; begar, my lore, de taut o' de occasione, o' de musketa, o' de cannona, o' de pika, de bullet, an de sworda, so run in my heada, dat begar me could do no tinga.

76 GEORGE VILLIERS, SECOND DUKE OF BUCKINGHAM

Lord. Ay, my Lord, I don't doubt of that. Your Lordship's most humble servant. [*Exit Lord.*
General. Begar, now dis be one very pretty tinga. Me beata de enemy like de great Generalla, like de man o' de conducta, an begar because me no born in Englanda, begar, de Englishman laff at me. Odsoona, de be de straingia natioon in de varld. [*Exit*

The basis of the humor in the farce, as the above quotations illustrate, is Buckingham's talent for personal ridicule. Grammont wrote, "His particular talent consisted in turning into ridicule whatever was ridiculous in other people, and in taking them off, even in their presence, without their perceiving it."[27] The contemporary accounts of Feversham from other sources confirm Buckingham's version of his speech and personality, but Buckingham's eye for specific detail is particularly sharp. And, of course, Buckingham exaggerated these qualities for humorous effect. Buckingham's irony in the farce is severe—more so than in most of his nondramatic personal satires. The addition of the allegation of sexual impotence at the end is uncharacteristically savage, and the dramatic form permits Buckingham to exploit the possibilities for irony more effectively than in his nondramatic pieces: here he can make Feversham condemn himself out of his own mouth.

Blank-Verse Heroic Fragment

The last of Buckingham's dramatic works is an incomplete heroic play which covers the first thirty-seven pages of his commonplace book, and which exists nowhere else. The fragment includes all of the first act of the play and the first scene of the second. It seems fairly certain that Buckingham was working on this play at the time of his death and that his death prevented his completing it.[28]

The hero of the play is Theodoric, king of the Ostrogoths (454–526), who in the years 488–93 invaded Italy and established a Gothic monarchy with its capital at Ravenna. The play is set just before the invasion; Theodoric's father, Theomirus, is attempting to unite all the Gothic nations in Gaul to take part on his side. The army of the Ostrogoths has besieged Euric, king of the Visigoths, in his capital city (probably Toulouse, but unnamed in the fragment) near Narbonne.

Before the play begins, Theodoric has managed to slip into the besieged city and to meet the beautiful Princess Amalzonta, daughter of King Euric, and he has fallen in love with her. Returning home, he has proposed to his father that he marry Amalzonta and unite the two Gothic nations, but Theomirus has refused.[29]

The play opens with Theodoric, disguised as a Roman and accompanied by his servant, Totilas, in the house of Liberius, a Visigoth nobleman who was captured by the Ostrogoths but has now been released. When Liberius goes to inform the king of his release, Theodoric explains to Totilas that a few days before, in the confusion of a night attack, he became lost. Knowing that he would be thought dead, he has disguised himself and has now managed to return to the city in the company of Liberius, hoping to see Amalzonta again and

> To tell her who I am, and what my busines
> To cast my fortune liberty and life franckly into her hands
> And as befits one totally subdued
> To yield myselfe to mercy, & not stand in composition (16)

Now a Visigoth gentleman enters, and, in response to a question from Theodoric, tells him that Amalzonta is betrothed to Torrismond, the son of Count Liberius, Theodoric's host. The news so discomposes Theodoric that he is barely able to preserve his disguise. The three men exit separately.

Next King Euric, Count Liberius, and the Lady Eudoxia, a friend of the princess's, enter. Liberius begins to tell the king about his release from Theomirus when a Visigoth captain enters to report a new Ostrogoth attack. The king acknowledges with alarm that he has sent the princess, guarded by a troop of cavalry under the command of Torrismond, to Narbonne for safety until the siege is lifted. Another captain enters to report that the Ostrogothic invaders have attacked the princess's party, causing heavy casualties. The remnant of the troop, still under Torrismond's command, is holding off the enemy until help can be sent.

Act 2 opens in the camp of Theomirus. The king, his queen, and his nobles are in the royal tent, gathered around an empty bier which represents Theodoric, supposed dead. Theomirus swears on the soul of Theodoric that if Euric or any member of his family falls into his hands, he will sacrifice them that very day upon the tomb of

Theodoric. He requires his wife, Fredegonda, and all his nobles to swear to execute the oath if he himself dies before it can be carried out.

Here the fragment ends. Although we can never know the outcome Buckingham had planned or what the overall success of the play might have been, we can see that suspense has been nicely built into the existing fragment. It seems likely that both Amalzonta and Torrismond would have fallen into the hands of Theomirus. How Theodoric would hear of their capture and his efforts to return to his father's camp and free the princess would have formed the substance, or part of it, of the remaining unwritten acts.

The first act is given over entirely to exposition: first Theodoric's explaining to Totilas (and, of course, to the audience) how he got where he is, and second the reports to Euric and his court about the situation of the princess. Such exposition is necessary to nearly all Restoration heroic drama, which often takes its plots from obscure histories and romances. In this play Buckingham accomplishes the exposition with grace, brevity, and interest.

One possible logical flaw in the fragmentary plot involves the character of Arsames, the courtier and diplomat who accompanied the disguised Theodoric into Euric's capital the first time. Theodoric's story as told to Totilas implies that he has revealed his identity and plans since the night attack to Arsames:

> Him you know how I persuaded, or how
> rather forced t' obtayne the Count Liberius
> His freedom
> (Which waighty grounds of state made very reasonable)
> And recommended mee to him at his parting
> as a considerable Roman gentleman
> and bound for Italy to passe along with him (15)

But if Arsames knows that Theodoric is alive, how could he keep that information from the sorrowing king and queen? How could he take part in the oath to avenge Theodoric's death on Euric and any member of his family, knowing that Theodoric is alive and loves Amalzonta?

Knowing the generally flat quality of Buckingham's blank verse in his emendations to Beaumont's and Fletcher's *Philaster*, we might expect that the weakest quality of this heroic play would be its style.

In fact, however, the style of the play is respectable, given the fact that it is unfinished. Naturally, it contains many passages of exposition. But even in such passages the naturalness of the dialogue and the freedom from the kind of meticulous counting of syllables which sometimes mars *The Restauration* are welcome.

There is also some of the bombast which, to twentieth-century readers, at least, is the characteristic fault of most Restoration heroic drama:

> *Totilas.* The sequel I can easily conceive
> You fell in love with her.
> *Theodoric.* So far thou mayest
> But how in love thou canst no more
> conceive, then you conceivest the nature
> of infinity, there's nothing but negations can
> expresse it, that 'twas a love unlike all
> love before. (7)

This fault Buckingham shares with many contemporary playwrights. But it is surprising to see such empty heroics in the work of the man who mocked them so thoroughly in *The Rehearsal*.

In several places in the fragment Buckingham's imagery provides both compression of expression and elevation of tone. Some of the best figurative language occurs in the speeches assigned to Theomirus, whom Buckingham endows with great force as he struggles to divert into revenge his grief for the supposed death of Theodoric. The metaphor of a damned stream in the following lines is characteristically vigorous: "Since Euric has thus rashly stopt the current / of my revenge on cruell Odoacer / It shall overflow, and drowne Him and his Country" (33). And the use of a knife or sword as the implicit vehicle of the following metaphor, reinforced by the implicit pun on "mettle," is suitable for a warrior-king:

> Fredegond, no more
> The heat of this affliction has enough
> Softened the noble metall of our courage,
> Tis time to strike it into forme and edge,
> And harden it again, lets to the business. (34)

Thus the style is sometimes quite good. If the play had been completed, it might have amplified its author's reputation.

As we have seen repeatedly in our examination of Buckingham's writings, comedy was the literary mode to which his talents naturally led him. Even such a slight and limited piece as *Sedgmoor Rehearsed* demonstrates how readily he could create ridiculous characters and comic dialogue. *The Country Gentleman*, insofar as it is his work, shows the same ability with greater range. In his revision of *The Chances* he designed, in Don John and the second Constantia, a pair of more complex comic characters and some witty dialogue better than that in many Restoration comedies. In serious drama, on the other hand, Buckingham always worked at a disadvantage. He seems not to have known how to be serious without being inflexibly so—or being unintentionally comic, as he sometimes was in *The Restauration*. Because it suggests that at the end of his life Buckingham was still developing his talents and might have been learning to write a more believable heroic style, the untitled fragment is particularly interesting.

Chapter Four
The Rehearsal

Buckingham's greatest work, the burlesque entitled *The Rehearsal*, was first performed on 7 December 1671. Apparently the play was written collaboratively by Buckingham with Martin Clifford and Samuel Butler, both of whom served him as secretaries, and with Thomas Sprat, his chaplain; there may have been other collaborators as well. It was originally written in the early 1660s and, according to some accounts, was ready for production in the summer of 1665, but the closing of the theaters that summer because of the plague prevented its production. When Buckingham's interest in his project returned, he made a number of major changes in the play.[1]

Essentially *The Rehearsal* is a burlesque—that is, a humorous imitation—of a form of drama which today is almost never seen on the stage, the Restoration heroic drama. For about twenty years, the heroic drama dominated the serious stage in England. It was characterized by extravagant spectacle, by violent emotional conflict, by impossibly heroic central characters, and by dialogue written in the highest style. Set in such romantically far-off places as Mexico, India, or Spain, the plays described great military heroes torn by complex conflicts between love and honor—love for the heroine, and honor in the form of loyalty to a king or country or a friend. The plays were written in iambic pentameter couplets, known since as "heroic couplets" because of their association with the form.[2] The principal author of heroic dramas in the 1660s and 1670s was the poet laureate, John Dryden, and his plays are naturally prominent among those which are burlesqued in Buckingham's farce. But many other plays are also explicitly satirized, and since the satire in *The Rehearsal* really reflects on the genre rather than on any single play or group of plays, it may be said to satirize any heroic drama, whether it is explicitly parodied or not.[3] In addition, *The Rehearsal* burlesques scenes, lines, or situations in other kinds of plays as well, whether heroic or not, if Buckingham and his collaborators found them ridiculous, illogical, or in poor taste.

The structure of *The Rehearsal* is fairly complex, for it incorporates one play within a larger one. The inner play, an untitled heroic drama supposedly written by Mr. Bayes, the playwright, is the real burlesque of the heroic drama. The outer play is a farce constructed around dialogue between Mr. Bayes and other characters—Mr. Smith and Mr. Johnson, two gentlemen whom Bayes has invited to his rehearsal, and the actors whom Bayes has engaged to perform his play.

The Inner Play

The inner play in *The Rehearsal* is Buckingham's mock version of a heroic drama. Its plot, insofar as it has one, involves two kings of Brentford (a western suburb of London), whose thrones are usurped by two of their attendants, the Physician and the Gentleman-Usher. Prince Pretty-man is in love with Cloris, and Prince Volscius with Parthenope. Prince Pretty-man believes himself to be the son of a fisherman, but he discovers that he is not. Lardella, a character who never appears on stage, has died, and there is a funeral procession for her, attended by the two usurpers. But we discover that Lardella is not dead, and her funeral turns into a banquet of celebration. The banquet is interrupted by the appearance of Drawcansir, the fierce hero, who seizes the usurpers' wine and drives them from the stage. Later, as the two unsurper-kings appear in state, surrounded by attendants, the two rightful kings of Brentford descend from the clouds, accompanied by music, and the usurpers steal away. All these revolutions of government are attended with bloody battles, and the revolutions of love and identity are accompanied by high-sounding rhetoric.

The plotlessness, incompleteness, and lack of dramatic consistency in the inner play are all intentional; they are intended to suggest similar qualities in Buckingham's targets. Also in the inner play are many burlesque imitations of the language, situations, and action of the contemporary stage, each of which is calculated to remind the audience of something familiar but to present it in a way which will show the absurdity or the flat tastelessness of the original.

Of these kinds of burlesque, no doubt the easiest for the playgoing audience to recognize were the verbal parodies. By these parodies Buckingham could remind his audience of specific lines in specific plays, and at the same time he could render those plays ridiculous.

An excellent example is his parody of the speeches of Almanzor, in Dryden's plays *The Conquest of Granada*, parts 1–2. Almanzor is the archetype of the hero of heroic drama, a great military hero, a passionate lover, a fiery-tempered man who again and again defies the power of kings and armies. In his essay "Of Heroic Plays," published as a preface to the two parts of *The Conquest*, Dryden defended the character of Almanzor by comparing him to the characters of Achilles in Homer's *Iliad* and of Rinaldo in Tasso's *Jerusalem Delivered*.[4] But whatever the precedents, Almanzor on the stage strains the audience's credulity and offers a ready subject for theatrical burlesque.[5]

For example, in the second part of *The Conquest of Granada*, the following dialogue takes place:

> *Almahide.* Who dares to interrupt my private Walk?
> *Almanzor.* He who dares love, and for that love must dy,
> And, knowing this, dares yet love on, am I.

In Bayes's play, Drawcansir, who parodies Almanzor, makes his first entrance during the banquet held by the two usurper-kings to celebrate Lardella's escape from death. His entrance is followed by the following dialogue:

> *King Physician.* What man is this, that dares to
> disturb our Feast?
> *Drawcansir.* He that dares drink, and for that drink
> dares dye,
> And, knowing this, dares yet drink on, am I.
> (4. 1. 220–24)

In the first part of *The Conquest of Granada*, Almanzor threatens a rival as follows:

> Thou dar'st not marry her while I'm in sight;
> With a bent brow thy Priest and thee I'le fright:
> And in that Scene
> Which all thy hopes and Wishes should content,
> The thought of me shall make thee impotent.

Bayes's Drawcansir makes a similar but more humorous threat in Buckingham's farce: "Who e'er to gulp one drop of this dares think / I'le stare away his very pow'r to drink" (4. 1. 296–97). Sheer force of will is an important element in the character of Almanzor, as well as in the character of Bayes's imitation of him. Almanzor epitomizes this quality in the following lines: "Spight of my self I'le Stay, Fight, Love, Despair; / And I can do all this, because I dare" (*Conquest of Granada*, part 2, act 2, scene 3). Drawcansir's version sums up his character even more succinctly: "I drink, I huff, I strut, look big and stare; / And all this I can do, because I dare" (4. 1. 248–49). These passages illustrate the way Buckingham's parody works. It retains the high style of the original, but it substitutes for the high subject a "lower" subject, which makes the style look ridiculous. For example, whereas Almanzor's daring is exerted to make his love possible—he dares to love even when love may cause his death—Drawcansir exerts the same force of will in order to drink.[6]

Great similes and metaphors provide much of the grandeur of great literature, but like truculent dialogue, they may read better on the page than they sound on the stage. In Dryden's *Conquest of Granada*, part 2, Almahide compares herself and Boabdelin in adversity to a pair of turtledoves in a storm; the turtledove, a standard symbol of love in European poetry, adds tenderness and pathos to her declaration:

> So two kind turtles, when a storm is nigh,
> Look up; and see it gath'ring in the Skie:
> Each calls his Mate, to shelter in the Groves,
> Leaving, in murmures, their unfinished Loves:
> Perch'd on some drooping Branch, they sit alone,
> And Cooe, and hearken to each others moan.

Our reaction to the plight of the separated turtledoves is conditioned by our traditional anthropomorphic acceptance of them as symbols of human emotion. To burlesque Dryden's simile, Buckingham substitutes for the turtledoves mating pigs:

> So Boar and Sow, when any storm is nigh,
> Snuff up, and smell it gath'ring in the Sky;
> Boar beckins Sow to trot in Chestnut Groves,
> And there consummate their unfinish'd Loves:
> Pensive in mud they wallow all alone,
> And snore and gruntle to each other's moan. (4. 1. 358–63)

As we read Buckingham's burlesque simile we feel mirth rather than pity, not only because of our feelings about pigs—that they are dirty, fat, and ugly, and that, in an anthropomorphic way analogous to our feelings about turtledoves, pigs symbolize a carnal side of ourselves—but also because in Buckingham's simile the "loves" are consummated rather than "unfinished."

In Dryden's *Tyrannick Love*, a heroine, Berenice, imagines her soul, liberated by death, remaining the constant companion of her still living lover. The image of the turtledove is again a natural simile:

> My earthy part—
> Which is my Tyrants right, death will remove,
> I'le come all Soul and Spirit to your Love
> With silent steps I'le follow you all day;
> Or else before you, in the Sun-Beams, play.
> I'le lead you thence to melancholy Groves,
> And there repeat the Scenes of our past Loves.
>
> And when at last, in pity, you will dye,
> I'le watch your Birth of Immortality:
> Then, Turtle-like, I'le to my Mate repair;
> And teach you your first flight in open Air.

It is not difficult to imagine a scene in which this consolation delivered bravely by a woman condemned to death, would move an audience to tears. But when Buckingham wishes to ridicule the passage, he does so readily by substituting a bumble-bee ("humble-bee," in the language of his time) for the turtledove and by changing Berenice's simile ("turtlelike") to an actual transmigration of the soul:

> Since death my earthly part will thus remove
> I'le come a Humble Bee to your chaste love.
> With silent wings I'll follow you, dear Couz;
> Or else, before you, in the Sun-beams, buz.
> And when to Melancholy Groves you come,
> An Airy Ghost, you'le know me by my Hum;
> For sound, being Air, a Ghost does well become. (4. 1. 143–49)

Buckingham's parodies of Dryden's similes do not always depend, as his parodies of the heroic rant do, on the originals' being ridiculous. Berenice's desire to be reunited in spirit with her lover after her death is a natural, though exalted, wish; and the image of the soul as a bird is common in all Christian literature. But the parody is funny, and to an audience who would be reminded of the tears it had shed at *Tyrannick Love*, it would be doubly funny.

Buckingham's prologue to *The Rehearsal* emphasizes that his purpose is to show audiences "What stuff it is in which they took delight" (1. 6), and most critics, taking their cue from the prologue, have seen the play simply as an attack on the contemporary stage. Certainly there was plenty on the contemporary stage that deserved attack, and as the passages of Drawcansir's ranting quoted above amply demonstrate, Buckingham could use parody very effectively for that purpose. But some of our delight in parody comes simply from the pleasant surprise of recognition. Audiences could laugh at the humble-bee without denying themselves the ability to feel the tenderness of the original ghost and turtledove. It is therefore not as surprising as some critics have supposed that Restoration audiences could enjoy both *The Rehearsal* and the heroic drama.[7]

Not all the humor in the inner play is derived from direct parody of other plays. Many of the situations in Bayes's play are burlesques of situations which occurred in any number of serious dramas, here rendered burlesque by being lowered in tone. For example, the precisely logical dialogue between the Gentleman-Usher and the Physician as to whether they have been overheard by the rightful kings of Brentford—"I divided the question into when they heard, / what they heard, and whether they heard or no" (2. 4. 15–16)—is not a verbal parody of any particular play, but a burlesque of similarly logical reasoning in many dramas.[8] The scene in which Prince Volscius, unable to decide whether to stay in town and follow the impulse of his love for Parthenope or to join the army in Knightsbridge as honor requires, stands with one boot on and one off (3. 5. 80–103) could be expected to remind contemporary audiences of all the conflicts between love and honor which form the substance of the heroic drama. Volscius's falling in love at first sight with Parthenope is also an exaggerated version of a frequent motif on the contemporary stage, not only in the heroic drama, but in the comedies as well.[9]

The Rehearsal also mocks much of the spectacle which was beginning to dominate the Restoration stage. Surely the most spectacular of these visual burlesques must have been the descent of the two kings of Brentford in clouds, accompanied by three Fiddlers (5. 1. 42ff.). The use of machinery to "fly" actors and scenes was one new development on the Restoration stage.[10] The dances and masques which did so much to enliven the seventeenth-century stage are parodied in the dance of dead soldiers in act 2, scene 5 and the eclipse-dance of the sun, moon, and earth in act 5, scene 1. The "great Scene" in which Bayes brings on stage two kings, four cardinals, two princes, three ladies, and numerous Heralds and Serjeants at Arms mocks those scenes of spectacle which crowd all lavish productions in all eras.[11]

Bayes's play is, then, a sustained burlesque of all that Buckingham and his collaborators found amusing or objectionable in the contemporary theater. In an age which loved all forms of literary humor, this piece is completely in the spirit of the age, but it is remarkable for its energy, good humor, and variety.

The Outer Play

The outer play of *The Rehearsal* gives the whole its distinctive character and makes it the work of genius that it is. This superstructure makes the play more than a series of witty insults to other playwrights and more than an expression of personal taste; *The Rehearsal* becomes, by means of the outer play, both a statement and an exemplar of an artistic doctrine.

Critical assumptions. The artistic and critical ideas embodied in *The Rehearsal* are not original with Buckingham. Quite the contrary, they were by his time literally ancient, having their roots in the works of Aristotle and Horace, the greatest of the Greek and Latin critical theorists. Central to this body of theory was the idea that any literary work should both delight and instruct its audience—that it should be, in Horace's Latin phrase, *dulce et utile*, "sweet and useful."[12] The writer, in this view, has no right to occupy the time of his reader or audience unless he profits them in some way—teaches them something. On the other hand, a work of art which is merely didactic loses its audience; therefore, Horace advises the writer (and generations of critics and authors repeated and refined his advice) to mingle delight with instruction so thoroughly that the two cannot be distinguished, so that the reader or viewer relishes the pleasure and at the same time learns the lesson.

In order to produce this mingled pleasure and instruction, writers in the Horatian and Aristotelian tradition (here called the "classical" tradition as a convenient, if at times misleading, term)[13] observed certain other principles. The first of these principles was that a work of art should imitate nature. By "nature" was meant not just flowers and birds, as in the phrase "nature poetry," but anything in creation.

For a playwright, "nature" means, above all else, "human nature." One's characters must be drawn from life. The audience's pleasure arises from its recognition, in the characters presented to it on the stage, of qualities it has observed, but perhaps not consciously noted, in persons encountered in real life. Alexander Pope, in his great critical treatise *An Essay on Criticism* (1711), summarized this first principle by saying that nature is "at once the source, and end, and test of art."[14] Nature is the source of art because the writer learns about his subject by studying nature. It is the end, in the sense of "goal," of art because the writer strives to have everything in his work resemble something in nature, in real life. And Nature is the test of art because when we judge a work of art we ask whether it is a successful (lifelife) imitation of nature.

Thus, according to classical theory, the great writer must be a gifted firsthand observer of nature who presents to mankind accurate images of what the rest of us see but may seldom notice. Since the greatest writers have always been such observers, the writer who wishes to know how to imitate nature successfully can learn a great deal by observing the practice of the greatest writers of the past. It is for this reason that writers in the classical tradition were conscious and respectful of that tradition. They believed that to know the works of the greatest writers of the past and to follow the examples such writers have set no more limits the originality of a modern writer than a consciousness of past discoveries in science limits the originality of a scientist. Indeed, since according to this tradition the writer, like the scientist, is an observer of nature, it is logical that in both fields a practitioner learn what he can from earlier observers. Thus Horace urges his reader to study the great Greek writers,[15] and Pope insists that the writer "know well each Ancient's proper Character."[16]

The classical tradition includes not only writers but critics. These critics have, by diligent study of the most successful works of literature, formulated certain principles, which the critics of the Restoration and eighteenth century called, simply, "The Rules." These rules were not listed in a single place; rather, they were principles enunciated in passing in the works of numerous writers such as those already cited. And of course they did not have the force of law; a great writer could break them with impunity, but he did so because he knew that he was achieving the great goal (the imitation of nature) in a new way. Once again, Pope puts the principle succinctly: "Moderns, beware! Or if you must offend / Against the Precept, ne'er transgress its End."[17] The rules were not imposed arbitrarily, but drawn, like the principles of physics, from the observation of nature. They had therefore great authority, and were not to be violated lightly.

Besides being conscious of nature and tradition, the writer in the classical tradition hoped to endow his work with other qualities which the critics of the time thought valuable. These included, but were not limited to, unity and variety, art, reason, and wit.

Unity and variety go together. A work must have enough variety in it to keep it from being monotonous, yet enough unity to give it coherence. The incidents in a plot must naturally be varied, for if they are not, the plot is repetitive, but at the same time it is necessary that they hold together if the story of the play is to be understood.

Reason is the same as logic. Everything in a work of art ought to "make sense." The work should be coherent. The critical requirement of reason should not be misunderstood as requiring that every work of art present an expository argument, or that characters in fiction or drama speak in syllogisms; to require that would break the more important rule that art "follow nature."

To Restoration critics, wit in writing was a combination of acutely perceptive observation with strikingly effective expression. A man of wit, like a poet, perceives clearly something in nature which most of us have never noticed. And, like a poet, he expresses his observations with such facility of language that we are immediately convinced of their truth. But in addition, wit has in it an element of surprise: a witty observation or remark has the sudden, exciting force of an unmediated thought. Because the delight produced by surprise is very compelling, critics of the period found it necessary to distinguish carefully between true wit, which consists in the association of thought and expression, and false wit, which is only playing with words—puns, for example, or riddles.

Art, finally, is the successful arrangement of all these elements in a unified whole which achieves the great twin goals of delight and instruction. Buckingham and his collaborators, in creating *The Rehearsal*, strove to fashion a work of art which would both teach how a play should be written—that it should delight and instruct, that it should imitate nature, that it should follow the authority of ancient authors and critical rules, and that it should incorporate order, variety, reason, wit, and art—and exemplify those principles.

  Action. The action of the outer play of *The Rehearsal* can quickly be summarized. In the opening scene, Mr. Smith, who has just arrived in London from the country, meets Mr. Johnson, a friend who lives in the city. They begin to discuss public affairs, then switch to a conversation about the theater, in which Johnson tells Smith that the plays performed recently are "such hideous, monstrous things, that it has almost made me forswear the Stage." As they talk, Mr. Bayes, a playwright, passes on his way to a dress rehearsal of his latest play. Johnson introduces Bayes to Smith, Bayes invites both men to the rehearsal, and they accompany him there. For the remainder of the play, the three men watch the rehearsal and comment on it. Bayes exhibits all of the qualities of his play which he thinks deserve admiration, but Johnson and Smith are increasingly disgusted, and eventually they leave before the rehearsal ends. When Bayes runs after them, the actors seize the opportunity to leave, too, so that when Bayes returns he finds no one there. He resolves to abandon writing for the theater and become a satirist against the taste of the town, which has not appreciated him.

The names "Smith" and "Johnson," two of the commonest in England, seem intended to suggest that these men are representative of the playgoing public. The commentary on the rehearsal between them and Bayes is designed to serve the artistic goal of instruction—that is, to help the audience to see how the parody in the inner play works. John Harold Wilson, in his biography of Buckingham, writes, "The London play-going public was so small that a play was rarely presented at either of the two theatres for more than three or four performances. Afterwards it was revived from time to time at intervals of six months or so. A popular play became as familiar as an old shoe, and parodies on it were instantly recognized."[18] Wilson's account of London theatrical practices during the Restoration is completely accurate, but we can see evidence in *The Rehearsal* that demonstrates that the parodies were not always instantly recognized. If they were, there might have been less need of the outer play. For one of the functions which Bayes serves is simply to call attention clearly to what the inner play is parodying. For example, before the simile of the Humble Bee, we have this dialogue:

> *Bayes.* And what do you think now I fancy her to make Love like, here, in the paper?
> *Smith.* Like a Woman: what should she make Love like?
> *Bayes.* O' my word you are out tho, Sir; I gad, you are.

Smith. What then? Like a man?
Bayes. No, Sir; like a Humble Bee.
Smith. I confess, that I should not have fancy'd. (4. 1. 123–28)

The idea that a woman writing a letter in verse would "make love... like a Humble Bee" seems perfectly absurd. Bayes's statement prepares us to recognize the foolishness of what is to follow. It may also cause us to overlook a distinction between the parody and its target, for whereas Lardella's verses speak of a literal transmigration of the soul to the body of a bee ("I'le come a Humble Bee to your Chaste love"), Dryden's *Tyrannick Love* used a simile ("Then, Turtle-like, I'le to my Mate repair"). It is fair, perhaps, to say that Lardella makes love like a humble bee, but it would be unfair to say that Berenice "makes love like a turtle-dove." When Bayes presents his song modeled on the contemporary "Farewel, fair Armida" he says, "'Tis to the Tune of Farewel, fair *Armida*, on Seas, and in battels, in Bullets, and all that" (3. 1. 107–8). Bayes's line alerts the audience to what they will hear parodied, so that they can keep the original in mind as they hear the parody. Before the masque of Luna, Orbis, and Sol in act 5, scene 1, Bayes says, "Why, the truth is, I took the first hint for this out of a Dialogue, between *Phoebus* and *Aurora* in the *Slighted Maid*: which by my troth, was very pretty; but I think, you'l confess this is a little better" (ll. 277–80). Regardless of the familiarity of the targets of parody, an audience in the theater is not like a reader, who can put the parody and the work it mocks before him at once and compare them. Buckingham must have known that to rely on the memories and quick wits of his auditors would have been to throw away many of his best effects. Therefore Bayes's comments, though they appear casual or random, help the audience recognize what it is seeing. In every case the comment precedes the part of the play to which it refers, so that the audience first hears what it will see and then sees it, like a class whose professor is making an audiovisual presentation.

But Buckingham was not content simply with having his witticisms recognized. His instructional purpose in this play is concealed in keeping with the injunction to mingle instruction with delight, but it is strong. The audience must not only recognize that contemporary plays are being mocked, but must be able to relate the mockery to the critical principles which in the inner play, and by extension in the contemporary theater, are violated.

For this purpose, the dialogue between Bayes and Smith and Johnson is essential. It is true that sometimes Bayes can—unknowingly—explain the standards which condemn him. When he introduces the two kings of Brentford, he explains that he has created them as a pair for the sake of novelty—and at the same time he alludes to the critical principle he is violating: "Why? because it's new; and that's it I aim at. I despise your Johnson and Beaumont, that borrow'd all they writ from Nature: I am for fetching it purely out of my own fancy, I" (2. 1. 61–64). Beaumont and Jonson imitated nature, as a writer should do; Bayes arrogantly supposes that he can find in his own imagination ("fancy") better materials than external reality can supply. But Bayes cannot always articulate the standards he violates, for to have him do so would betray an awareness of these standards which would be incompatible with his ignorance and foolishness. Here the dialogue between Bayes and Smith and Johnson is important. For example, Smith articulates the same principle—follow nature—when, after Bayes explains that the battle over the usurpation of the throne follows the usurpation itself, he says sarcastically, "O, I conceive you: that, I swear, is very natural" (2. 4. 97).

Bayes's play also violates the standard of reason or logic. Johnson and Smith, by pointing to elements of illogic, help the audience to understand why logic is necessary. For example, the following dialogue takes place in the inner play:

> *Usher.* The grand question is, whether they heard us whisper? which I divide thus.
> *Physician.* Yes, it must be divided so indeed.

Watching this scene, Smith comments, "That's very complaisant, I swear, Mr. Bayes, to be of another man's opinion, before he knowes what it is." Obviously we see Smith's irony; we understand that what he calls "complaisancy" is simple absurdity, illogic. But Bayes takes him at his word, and replies, "Nay, I bring in none, here, but welbred persons, I assure you" (2. 4. 8–14). Bayes similarly misses the point in this exchange:

> *Drawcansir.* He that dares drink, and for that drink dares dye,
> And, knowing this, dares yet drink on, am I.
> *Johnson.* That is, Mr. Bayes, as much to say, that tho he would rather die than not drink, yet he would fain drink for all that too.

> *Bayes.* Right; that's the conceipt on't.
> *Johnson.* 'Tis a marvellous good one, I swear. (4. 1. 222–27)

Johnson's paraphrase of Drawcansir's ranting speech shows how it is a tautology. If he "dares drink, and for that drink dares dye," then obviously he "dares yet drink on." If we missed some of the redundancy in Buckingham's parody of Dryden's lines in *The Conquest of Granada* (and—by extension—in the original), Johnson's paraphrase may help us to see it. The illogic in a metaphor may not readily be apparent to someone who is not examining it rigorously, so that the dialogue following Bayes's metaphors helps to explain them:

> *Physician.* Sir, to conclude, the place you fill, has more than amply exacted the Talents of a wary Pilot, and all these threatning storms, which, like impregnate Clouds, hover o'er our heads, will (when they once are grasp'd but by the eye of reason) melt into fruitful showers of blessings on the people.
> *Bayes.* Pray mark that Allegory. Is not that good?
> *Johnson.* Yes; that grasping of a storm, with the eye, is admirable. (2. 1. 30–37)

One of the major faults of Bayes's play is that it lacks unity and coherence. He seems to insert any element that strikes his fancy, without regard to how it might fit together with any other element. Preoccupied with the immediate effect on the audience of a scene or line, Bayes neglects the total fabric of his play. The dialogue between him and the other two gentlemen emphasizes this incoherence. Thus after the scene of "witty" banter between Prince Pretty-man and Tom Thimble, we have the following dialogue:

> *Bayes.* Ha, there he has hit it up to the hilts, I gad! How do you like it now, Gentlemen? Is not this pure Wit?
> *Smith.* 'Tis snip snap, Sir, as you say; but, methinks, not pleasant, nor to the purpose, for the Play does not go on.
> *Bayes.* Play does not go on? I don't know what you mean: why, is not this part of the Play?
> *Smith.* Yes, but the Plot stands still.
> *Bayes.* Plot stand still! why, what a Devil is the Plot good for, but to bring in fine things?

> *Smith.* O, I did not know that before.
> *Bayes.* No, I think you did not: nor many things more, that I am Master of. Now, Sir, I gad, this is the bane of all us Writers: let us soar but never so little above the common pitch, I gad, all's spoil'd; for the vulgar never understand it, they can never conceive you, Sir, the excellency of these things. (3. 1. 66–82)

Here both sides advance their views of the problem of unity. Bayes does not see it as a problem. The plot of his play is simply a clothesline on which he can hang his "fine things"—his sentimental metaphors, his passages of witty banter, and his monologues about love and honor. The fact that they do not fit together does not bother him, because he does not have the capacity to imagine that they *could* fit together. To Smith and Johnson, on the other hand, no amount of bombast or wit or sentiment can compensate for the incoherence of an ill-managed plot. A work of art must have unity, a single design, if it is to be pleasing.

> *Bayes.* Mark how I make the horrour of his guilt confound his intellects; for he's out at one and t'other; and that's the design of this Scene.
> *Smith.* I see, Sir, you have a several design for every Scene.
> *Bayes.* I, that's my way of writing; and so Sir, I can dispatch you a whole Play, before another man, I gad, can make an end of his Plot. (3. 3. 30–36)

Because he does not concern himself with unity and writes a whole play simply as a series of scenes, without regard to how they fit together, Bayes can congratulate himself upon the speed with which he composes.

Although he disregards so many of the critical rules that we have thus far examined, Bayes does not write in complete disregard of rules. He has his own rules. Some of them are distortions of the traditional critical dogmas; others seem to be the arbitrarily composed products of his own imagination. His comments on the relationships between his practice and his "rules" help an audience to understand what they are seeing and remind them of the standards he violates.

First among Bayes's own critical principles is demand for originality. Thus he tells Smith and Johnson before the first scene of his play,

"Now, Sir, because I'll do nothing here that ever was done before, instead of beginning with a Scene that discovers something of the Plot, I begin this Play with a whisper." When the whispering scene has ended, he asks, "Now, Gentlemen, pray tell me true, and without flattery, is not this a very odd beginning of a Play?" The fact that Bayes equates "odd" with "original" indicates the nature of his misunderstanding of a key critical principle. Originality is something that is always valued in art, but writers in the classical tradition value originality in a carefully defined way. For them, originality consists not in doing "nothing ... that was ever done before," but in adapting what is always done to new circumstances and situations. If we believe, as writers in the classical tradition do, that the greatest ideas could not remain hidden from the greatest minds over many centuries, then we must infer that anything that has literally never been done before is not worth doing. What is odd is not original, but trivial.

In the view of writers and critics in the classical tradition, therefore, the best way for a writer to be original is to make himself familiar with the work of the great writers of the past. We have already noted the classical dogma requiring the writer to be familiar with the writings of the "ancients." Bayes is not ignorant of the ancients, but his knowledge is fragmentary, disorganized, and full of misunderstandings. Despite his claims of originality, he uses other writers not as a basis for his invention, but as substitutes for it:

> *Smith.* But pray, Mr. Bayes, among all your other Rules, have you no one Rule for invention?
> *Bayes.* Yes, Sir; that's my third Rule that I have here in my pocket.
> *Smith.* What Rule can that be, I wonder?
> *Bayes.* Why, Sir, when I have any thing to invent, I never trouble my head about it, as other men do; but presently turn over this Book, and there I have, at one view, all that *Perseus, Montaigne, Seneca's Tragedies, Horace, Juvenal, Claudian, Pliny, Plutarch's lives*, and the rest, have ever thought upon this subject: and so, in a trice, by leaving out a few words, or putting in others of my own, the business is done.
> (1. 1. 124–36)

The fact that Bayes boasts of this plagiarism as a means of "invention" shows that he understands neither invention nor originality.

We have already seen that another classical critical principle requires a careful balance between variety and unity in every work of art. Bayes misunderstands this principle, too. All his emphasis is on the need for variety, and he ignores entirely the need for dramatic unity. "The variety of all the several accidents," according to his theory, "are the things in Nature that make up the grand refinement of a Play" (1. 1. 230-32). In one scene of his play, Prince Pretty-man sees Cloris, falls in love with her—and immediately falls asleep. Bayes is triumphant: "Does not that, now, surprise you, to fall a sleep in the nick? His spirits exhale with the heat of his passion, and all that, and swop falls a sleep, as you see" (2. 3. 10-12). Of course, we, together with Smith and Johnson, see that Pretty-man's sleep is completely unnatural and, further, that it bears no relation to the overall design of the play (which really does not exist anyway). But to Bayes the fact that it is surprising is enough. As he says after he has had the goddess Pallas produce food and wine from her clothing, "the chief Art in Poetry is to elevate your expectation, and then bring you off in some extraordinary way" (4. 1. 217-19).

In his comments on the style of his play, too, Bayes shows a misunderstanding of classical principle. The principle of decorum, known since Horace, requires that the style of a work of literature be suited to its form and its subject. Thus tragedy, the highest dramatic form, is written in verse and in the highest available language. Comedy, a less exalted form, was written in everyday language and ordinarily in prose. Bayes's twisted understanding of the rule of decorum makes different requirements—all of them surprising, few of them really logical. His ideas of kingly style show no familiarity either with nature or with art:

    1 King. Did you observe their whisper, Brother King?
    2 King. I did; and heard, besides, a grave-bird sing, That they intend, sweet-heart, to play us pranks.
    Bayes. This, now, is familiar, because they are both persons of the same Quality.
    1 King. You must begin, *Mon foy.*
    2 King. Sweet Sir, *Pardonnes moy.*
    Bayes. Mark that: I makes 'em both speak *French,* to shew their breeding. (2.2. 5-9, 16-18)

Bayes's rule that "you must ever make a *simile*, when you are surpris'd; 'tis the new way of writing" (2. 3. 16) is equally bizarre.

In all these ways, therefore, the outer play of *The Rehearsal* provides a kind of gloss on the inner play, allowing the audience to appreciate the parody better than it otherwise could. But, of course, the outer play could not hold the attention of the audience if it were not entertaining in itself; and in fact, much of the entertainment in *The Rehearsal* lies not in the burlesque of the inner play but in the farce of the outer play.

All readers of the play have noticed that Smith and Johnson fool Bayes with their sarcastic comments—that they allow him to believe that they accept him and his play at his own estimation of their value, while in fact they are amused or disgusted. But previous critics have not noticed that the two characters, Smith and Johnson, although they are both men of taste and understanding, differ somewhat from one another.

Smith is newly arrived in London from the country. Like Sir Richard Plainbred, the title character of Buckingham's and Howard's *The Country Gentleman*, he is innocent of the corruptions which have taken hold in the city. He values honesty and plain-dealing; Johnson addresses him as "Honest Frank," and he tells Johnson, "I long to talk with you freely, of all the strange new things we have heard in the country." Johnson, on the other hand, is a town rake:

> *Smith.* Well; but how dost thou pass thy time?
> *Johnson.* Why, as I use to do; eat and drink as well as I can, have a she-friend to be private with in the afternoon, and sometimes see a Play.... (1. 1. 24–27)

It is characteristic of the rakes in Restoration comedy that they manipulate others for the sake of their own pleasures, and we shall see that Johnson resembles the other rakes in that respect.[19] Whereas Smith is intrigued by novelty, Johnson is sated with it: "And, by my troth, I have long'd as much to laugh with you, at all the impertinent, dull, fantastical things, we are tir'd out with here" (1. 1. 7–9). Thus whereas Smith wishes to talk freely with Johnson, Johnson wishes to laugh in mockery with Smith. The farce that follows involves a struggle between them as each seeks his own pleasure in the company of the other.

When Bayes passes, Johnson instantly sees an opportunity for laughter of the kind he enjoys.

> *Bayes.* Your most obsequious, and most observant, very servant, Sir.
> *Johnson.* God so, this is an Author: I'l fetch him to you.
> *Smith.* No, Pr'ythee let him alone.
> *Johnson.* Nay, by the Lord, I'l have him. *Goes after him.* Here he is. I have caught him. (1. 1. 49–54)

Smith asks Johnson to leave Bayes alone because his is not the kind of personality which derives pleasure from mockery of others. He can divine the kind of fun Johnson has in mind, and he is not interested in it. Furthermore, having heard Bayes's ridiculously fulsome greeting, he knows that the playwright's company and conversation will prevent the pleasure he himself desires—free, frank conversation with his friend, Johnson. But his regard for his friend is genuine and his temperament obliging, so that he decides, having heard Bayes's invitation to the rehearsal, that he would rather have Johnson's company, even with the discomfiting addition of Bayes's, than not have it at all:

> *Johnson.* [to Bayes] Sir, I confess, I am not able to answer you in this new way; but if you please to lead, I shall be glad to follow you; and I hope my friend will do so too.
> *Smith.* Sir, I have no business so considerable, as should keep me from your company. (1. 1. 79–83)

Of the character of Bayes we have already seen enough to know that he is a fool. Like the principal fools of all the Restoration comedies, he has a hyperactive imagination ("fancy"), enormous energy, very little judgment, and no self-awareness. His first speech about his play reveals the salient qualities of his mind:

I have a new one, in my pocket, that I may say is a Virgin; 't has never yet been blown upon. I must tell you one thing. 'Tis all new Wit; and tho I say it, a better than my last: and you know well enough how that took. In fine, it shall read, and write, and act, and plot, and shew, ay, and pit, box, and gallery, I gad, with any Play in *Europe.* This morning is its last Rehearsal, in their habits, and all that, as it is to be acted; and if you, and your friend will do it but the honour to see it in its Virgin attire; though, perhaps, it may blush, I shall not be asham'd to discover its nakedness unto you. (1. 1. 67–77)[20]

Bayes's metaphorical references to his play as "a Virgin" suggest a kind of prurience which is confirmed later in his boasts of having "talkt bawdy" to his actress mistress. But in addition, he uses the metaphor without logical coherence. He asks Smith and Johnson to "see it in its Virgin attire," but then proposes to "discover its nakedness unto you." The virgin of the metaphor cannot be both clothed and naked.

Except for the Players, who have very small roles in it, these three are the characters of the outer farce. As that farce progresses, Johnson manipulates events so that the unrestrained ego of Bayes and the frankness of Smith keep them always on the verge of an open clash, but never quite in one. Behind Bayes's back he reassures Smith that the two of them are laughing at the playwright. Fairly openly (since Smith sees this activity as part of the plot to exhibit Bayes), he reassures Bayes that Bayes and he, as sophisticated Londoners and theatergoers, understand what Smith does not: "Phoo! pr'ythee, *Bayes*, don't mind what he says: he is a fellow newly come out of the Country, he knows nothing of what's the relish, here, of the Town" (1. 1. 283–85). Johnson's statement to Bayes is, of course, true. But whereas Bayes naturally supposes that Smith is to be pitied for his lack of knowledge, we know that Johnson has already characterized the relish of the town to Smith as "dull and fantastical," and tiresome.

When the scene between the Gentleman-Usher and the Physician unfolds, both Smith and Johnson interrupt with questions. But Bayes takes Johnson's questions as well meant, Smith's as naive and irritating:

>   *Physician.* Sir, to conclude.
>   *Smith.* What, before he begins?
>   *Bayes.* No, Sir; you must know, they had been talking of this a pretty while without.
>   *Smith.* Where? in the Tyring-room?
>   *Bayes.* Why ay, Sir. He's so dull! Come, speak again. (2. 1. 24–29)

The line "He's so dull!" is addressed to Johnson, with whom Bayes is beginning to imagine himself in a kind of conspiracy to expose Smith's country dullness.

A few minutes later, Smith tells Johnson that he does not enjoy the game: "Pox on't but there's no Pleasure in him: he's too gross a fool to be laugh'd at" (2. 1. 94–95). But Johnson, determined to prolong it, tries to provoke Bayes to jealousy by telling him that Smith is a rival writer. For the moment the provocation is unsuccessful. Rather than be envious, Bayes tries, in effect, to exchange recipes for composition with Smith: "Why, I'll tell you, now, what I do. If I am to write familiar things, as Sonnets to Armida, and the like, I make use of Stew'd Prunes only; but, when I have a grand design in hand, I ever take Phisic, and let blood: for, when you would have pure swiftness of thought, and fiery flights of fancy, you must have a care of the pensive part. In fine, you must purge the Belly" (2. 1. 114–20). The analogy between literary composition and evacuation of the body is not original with Buckingham. In fact, it was a popular one among the Restoration court wits. Rochester used it in his "Epistolary Essay from M. G. to O. B. upon Their Mutual Poems" (1679), and Buckingham himself returned to it in his "Familiar Epistle to Mr. Julian, Secretary to the Muses" (1677).[21] In both poems the use of the image is much broader and more scatological than in *The Rehearsal*. But there is a common element in all of them, for in all cases bad poets are described as writing not to imitate nature, not to delight and instruct, but to rid themselves of a painful and noxious load—and by ridding themselves of it they inflict it on the rest of the world.

As the rehearsal progresses, Bayes feels an increasing solidarity with Johnson against Smith. He has been offended by Smith's question about whether the "plot does not go on" during the exchange between Pretty-man and Thimble, and he is offended again at Smith's questioning the idea that Tom Thimble's wife made up a song after she was dead (3. 1. 68–78, 93–100). Now he begins to feel that his play is a touchstone for wit, that it separates the witty man (e.g., Johnson) from the dullard (Smith): "Nay, nay, come, come, Mr. Johnson, I faith ... I know you have wit by the judgment you make of this Play; for that's the measure I go by; my Play is my Touchstone. When a man tells me such a one is a person of parts; is he so, say I? what do I do, but bring him presently to see this Play: If he likes it, I know what to think of him; if not, your most humble Servant, Sir, I'l no more of him upon my word, I thank you. I am *Clara voyant*, I gad" (3. 2. 130–39).

Smith's questions continue to irritate Bayes, but now he believes that he has an ally in Johnson—and Johnson does what he can to encourage this belief. Thus when Bayes insists that the two men admire the phrase, "Held the honour of your company," Johnson

The Rehearsal

replies, "I assure you, Sir, I admire it extreamly: I don't know what he does." Bayes, perhaps remembering that Smith is a rival poet, responds, "I, I, he's a little envious, but 'tis no great matter" (3. 5. 18–20). Now when Bayes is puzzled at how to answer Smith's questions, Johnson prompts him and thus becomes, in effect, a kind of collaborator:

> Smith. But pray, Mr. *Bayes*, is not this a little difficult, that you were saying e'en now, to keep an army thus conceal'd in *Knights-bridge*?
> Bayes. In Knights-bridge? stay.
> Johnson. No, not if the Inn-keepers be his friends.
> Bayes. His Friends! Ay, Sir, his intimate acquaintance; or else, indeed, I grant it could not be.
>
> Smith. Well, and where lyes the jest of that?
> Bayes. Ha? *Turns to Johnson.*
> Johnson. Why, in the Boots: where should the jest lie?
> Bayes. I Gad, you are in the right: it does Lie in the Boots— *Turns to Smith.* Your friend, and I know where a good jest lies, tho you don't Sir.
> Smith. Much good do't you, Sir. (3. 5. 29–35, 68–75)

Throughout the fourth act Bayes extorts praise from Johnson and airily dismisses questions from Smith. In the fifth act, the tension among the characters rises. Bayes has almost ceased to pay Smith the courtesy of a reply:

> Smith. Mr. *Bayes*, pray what is the reason that two of the Cardinals are in Hats, and the other in Caps?
> Bayes. Why, Sir, because—By Gad, I won't tell you. Your Country friend, Sir, grows so troublesome. (5. 1. 8–11)

And Smith is approaching violence in his disgust:

> Smith. Well, I can hold no longer, I must gag this rogue; there's no induring of him.
> Johnson. No, pr'thee make use of thy patience a little longer; let's see the end of him now. (5. 1. 115–18)

Even for Johnson himself the pleasure in the episode is diminishing. The dances and battles have become tedious with repetition. So when Bayes next leaves the stage, Johnson and Smith slip away.

What can Johnson's motive have been? In part, perhaps, we can accept his statements to Smith that he has wanted to display Bayes for his friend's amusement. But Smith has repeatedly protested that he is not amused. It may be that in part Johnson has been rebuking Smith for his curiosity about "the strange new things we have heard in the Country." Perhaps he has enjoyed showing his country friend why it is so easy to tire of novelty in the city. But his most important motive may simply have been the sense of superiority that he felt over both Bayes and Smith. While Bayes has been a fool and Smith has been disgusted, he, Johnson, has been in charge—allied with each against the other, gratifying a malicious sense of humor at the discomfiture of both. It is not much of a plot, for it has a carefully limited function to fulfill: it must keep the audience interested enough that they will be entertained, but the plot of the outer farce cannot be so exciting that it takes the audience's attention away from what it is learning about the theater from the inner play and the critical comments.

Personal Satire in *The Rehearsal*

As we have already seen, Buckingham lived in a time when vicious personal attacks were an accepted part of social, political, and literary life. In the relatively small society of England's political, economic, and cultural capital, references to the physical characteristics or personal habits of individuals were immediately recognizable and were considered fair play. Buckingham's contributions to *The Country Gentleman* and his nondramatic personal satires show that he was as willing to play this game as any of his contemporaries and that he was an able player. It is not surprising, therefore, that critics and scholars for three centuries have examined *The Rehearsal* in search of references to specific individuals—or that they have been convinced that they have found them.

Traditionally, the most widely accepted idea of a personal allusion in the play has been the supposition that Bayes, the chief character, represents John Dryden, the greatest poet of Buckingham's time. The reason for the supposition is easy enough to identify. The word "bays" is a synonym for the laurel crown, the classical symbol of poetic excellence. John Dryden was, at the time *The Rehearsal* was produced, the poet laureate of England. Obviously, the connection between the laurel of the laureate and the Bayes of the character's name made the identification a natural one.

Furthermore, Dryden was, as we have already seen, the leading author of heroic drama of his time. Of the thirty-seven plays which are overtly subjected to parody in *The Rehearsal*, eight (of which one, *The Assignation*, was not parodied in the original version produced for the stage in 1671, but was added in an expanded edition in 1675) are the work of Dryden. More of his plays than any other author's are mocked in *The Rehearsal*: for example, D'Avenant has three plays parodied, Sir Robert Howard four.

In the rough-and-tumble atmosphere of his age, Dryden's political and religious principles and his effective use of his pen in support of them had made him many enemies. For these enemies, the associations just mentioned were enough to make the identification of Dryden with Bayes an accepted fact, and from 1671 on, the name "Bayes" stuck firmly to Dryden in all controversial writing. By 1682, when Shadwell published *The Medal of John Bayes* (a virulently obscene attack on Dryden written in reply to Dryden's own attack on Shaftesbury entitled *The Medal*), it had become proverbial. As the legend grew and was elaborated, allegations about Dryden were made with the intention of making the similarities between him and Bayes more convincing. For example, in his preface to *The Medal of John Bayes*, Shadwell describes Dryden as trying to find the proper diet to make his writing flow more easily, as Bayes claims to do in *The Rehearsal* (2. 114–20; see above).[22] After the turn of the century, even friendly biographers of Dryden accepted the identification, and they sometimes discovered evidence that supported it.

For a modern student of *The Rehearsal* who wishes to discover whether Buckingham actually intended a caricature of Dryden's personal appearance and behavior, the problem becomes one of distinguishing between the legends which have grown up since the first performance of *The Rehearsal* (and are therefore tainted) and any evidence for real similarities between the character of Bayes and the personal characteristics of the historical Dryden. Although the amount of reliable information about Dryden is too small to make a truly conclusive determination possible, there is no convincing evidence that a personal satire against Dryden was intended.

The strongest evidence for the identification has always been the collateral stories, which have alleged that Bayes as he was acted on the stage mimicked Dryden's personal characteristics. Here is one editor's account of the matter:

> Not satisfied with parodying some of the most familiar passages in Dryden's plays, the Duke of Buckingham took considerable pains in teaching Lacy, who performed *Bayes*, to mimic the author in his manner of reciting them. Dryden was notoriously a bad reader, and had a hesitating and tedious delivery, which, skillfully imitated in lines of surpassing fury and extravagance, must have produced an irresistible effect upon the audience. The humour was enhanced by the dress, gesticulations, and byplay of the actor, which presented a close imitation of his original.[23]

So detailed are the circumstances, and so authoritative is the tone in which they are related, that it will certainly surprise most readers of this passage to discover that they are mostly drawn not from an eyewitness account but from the imaginations of this editor and his predecessors. The ultimate source for the ancedote is an account by Dean Francis Lockier, who was personally acquainted with Dryden. Here is Lockier's actual statement, as told to Joseph Spence: "It is incredible what pains he took with one of the actors, to teach him to speak some passages in Bays's part, in the Rehearsal, right."[23]

It is easy to see that Bell's account, cited earlier, has elaborated many of the details of Lockier's. Lockier says nothing of Lacy's wearing Dryden's clothes or imitating his manner of speaking. In fact, Lockier says nothing of Dryden at all: he says that Buckingham taught Lacy to speak the part correctly, but he does not say that he taught him to imitate any particular person. The connection with Dryden exists only in the minds of subsequent editors.

In addition, Lockier was not, as most biographers of Dryden have assumed he was, an eyewitness to the events he describes in this quotation. It is true that he was a friend of Dryden's, but he was much younger. He was born in 1668; one of his earliest anecdotes is his account of his meeting Dryden in 1685, when he was a young man of eighteen and Dryden was the established poet. Therefore Lockier was no more than three years old in the fall of 1671, when *The Rehearsal* was being prepared for the stage. It is impossible that he could have witnessed Buckingham's assisting Lacy with his part. Thus what at first looks like evidence is not an eyewitness account, and it does not link Dryden with Bayes. It evaporates upon examination.

Much the same is true of another traditional account, in Davies's *Dramatic Miscellanies* (1783). Davies says not only that Lacy was dressed in clothes like Dryden's, but that Buckingham and the earl of Dorset contrived to take Dryden to the theater for the first performance, so as to enjoy his discomfiture. But Davies wrote his account more than one hundred years after the events he describes, and, to his credit, he so qualifies his account with phrases like "it was said," "we may suppose," and "if we can trust to tradition," that we can see that even he thought his account dubious.[25]

Little is known today about Dryden's physical characteristics, personal habits, or mannerisms of speech or gesture, so that even if we knew what "stage business" Lacy used—and we do not—it would be difficult for us to judge whether or not he was trying to imitate Dryden. But if we examine the characteristics of Bayes on the stage, we find that he does not particularly resemble what little we know about Dryden.

For example, one of the principal characteristics of Mr. Bayes is the volubility and maniac energy of his talk. When he first crosses the stage, his greeting to Johnson and Smith is overelaborate and awkward: "Your most obsequious, and most observant, very servant, Sir." When Johnson asks him to do a favor, Bayes answers, "Sir, it is not within my small capacity to do favours, but receive 'em; especially from a person that does wear the honourable Title you are pleas'd to impose, Sir, upon this.—Sweet Sir, your servant" (1. 1. 49–50, 56–59). There is some evidence that Dryden's conversation was the very opposite of Bayes's. In his "Defense of an Essay of Dramatic Poesy," Dryden writes of himself, "My conversation is slow and dull; my humour saturnine and reserved: in short, I am none of those who endeavor to break jests in company, or make repartees."[26] Of course, it is possible that Dryden misunderstood himself and was unaware of the impression he made upon others, or that he was trying politely to deprecate his conversational wit. But his enemies, when they quoted the passage just cited, did so not to disagree with it, but to suggest that it understated the case. Other unfriendly accounts of Dryden's conversation suggest that he was not obsequiously polite or extensively voluble, but tactlessly blunt.[27]

Much has been made of Bayes's claimed connection with the actress who plays Amaryllis in the play. Bayes boasts to Smith and Johnson of his plans to seduce the actress and says he has already "talkt bawdy" to her. It has traditionally been thought that Dryden's own mistress was the actress Anne Reeve, and because Mrs. Reeve is known to have played the part of Esperanza in Dryden's *The Conquest of Granada*, Bayes's compliment to her, "bel Esperansa de ma vie," has seemed a clear dig at Dryden. But it is not at all clear that Mrs. Reeve was the poet's mistress, and since the phrase "esperansa de ma vie" is necessary to Bayes's double entendre, it need not be pointed at Dryden.

Bayes's claim that he "purges the body" with stewed prunes before writing has led one scholar to write that "Dryden's love of stewed prunes was extremely well known."[28] But this is wishful thinking, trying to make the identification stick. As we have already seen, the point of that exchange is the humorous analogy between defecation and bad writing which occurs in Restoration satires unconnected with Dryden.

Dryden's own recorded comments on the play are ambiguous. In his *Discourse Concerning the Original and Progress of Satire*, published in 1693, more than twenty years after the first performance of *The Rehearsal*, he wrote, "I answered not *The Rehearsal*, because I knew the author sat to himself when he drew the picture, and was the very Bayes of his own farce; because also I knew that my betters were more concerned than I was in that satire; and lastly, because Mr. Smith and Mr. Johnson, the main pillars of it, were two such languishing gentlemen in their conversation that I could liken them to nothing but to their own relations, those noble characters of men of wit and pleasure about the town."[29] In what sense did Dryden consider an "answer"—to the parodies of his plays, or to a personal attack upon himself? Who were Dryden's "betters" (social superiors) who were "more concerned"? And what have the characters of Smith and Johnson to do with any attack on him? Similarly, when Lockier says that Dryden "allowed the Rehearsal to have a great many good strokes in it; 'though so severe,' added he, 'upon myself,' " in what sense did Dryden think the play severe upon him—on his person or on his plays?

In any event, years of being called Bayes may have led Dryden eventually to suppose himself personally attacked in *The Rehearsal*, but as Robert Hume has pointed out, he seemed to show no immediate resentment. In the *Defense of the Epilogue*, written just two months after *The Rehearsal* was first performed, Dryden handsomely compliments Buckingham's revision of Fletcher's *The Chances. The Rehearsal* was staged by the King's Company, for which Dryden was the principal writer. It seems unlikely that the actors, dependent upon Dryden for their prosperity, would have taken part in a scheme to humiliate him.[30]

Bayes is a composite figure, in whom the stock Restoration stage fools make up the greatest part. Although we cannot ignore the tradition which equates him with Dryden, there is no evidence which proves conclusively—or even makes probable—the supposition that he is a personal caricature of the poet laureate.

A different kind of personal satire was suggested in 1974 by George McFadden in a well-researched article entitled "Political Satire in *The Rehearsal*."[31] McFadden hypothesized that the play may be not simply a burlesque of the heroic drama, but a carefully constructed satire, capable of easy interpretation by court insiders, on the political situation in England in 1671. In McFadden's interpretation, Bayes is not Dryden but Henry Bennet, earl of Arlington, Buckingham's archrival in the internal wars of the Cabal ministry. Arlington wore a black patch on his nose exactly like the one worn by Bayes after he injures his nose in act 2, scene 5, line 27, and in 1671 he had just outmaneuvered Buckingham in the matter of the command of the English army in the Netherlands (see chapter 1). According to McFadden, the two kings of Brentford are intended to satirize King Charles and his brother, James, duke of York, and their bowing and scraping to one another suggest the Country party's disagreements with the royal family over the succession to the throne.

McFadden's theory is an attractive one. It is always exciting to learn something new about a work we have thought we fully understood, and if *The Rehearsal* conceals a political satire beneath its theatrical burlesque, it is an even more complex and interesting work than we have supposed. McFadden's suggestion that the two kings of Brentford are representations of the king and the duke of York can be extended somewhat. For example, the two usurpers, the Physician and the Gentleman-Usher, may be intended to represent Sir William Coventry and his friend and colleague, Sir John Duncomb, whom Buckingham had attempted earlier to satirize in the suppressed play, *The Country Gentleman*. Bayes introduces their dialogue by telling Smith and Johnson that " 'tis a Discourse I over-heard once betwixt two grand, sober, governing persons" (2. 3. 57–58), and later, in the middle of the scene, he adds that " 'tother [the Gentleman-Usher] is the main Politician, and this [the Physician] is but his pupil" (2. 4. 32–33). Buckingham may have seen Coventry's maneuvers in the Privy Council on behalf of the duke of York's faction as a form of usurpation, so that presenting these two court gentlemen as usurpers would further the political allegory.[32] Prince Pretty-man, who is thought to be a fisherman's son but who is really the son of a king, and who fears that "he should be thought no bodies Son at all" (3. 4. 68–69), may represent King Charles's handsome illegitimate son, the duke of Monmouth, whose legitimacy was a matter of public concern in the disputes over the succession to the throne.

On the other hand, these resemblances are not systematic or sustained. Prince Pretty-man may resemble Monmouth in his good looks and in the uncertainty of his birth, but Pretty-man is peace-loving, whereas Monmouth at the time *The Rehearsal* was first presented was acting more like Drawcansir: in December 1670 his bullies had slit the nose of a member of Parliament in retaliation for a reckless riposte, and in February 1671 he and a group of carousing friends, accosted in Whetstone Park by a beadle named Peter Vernell, murdered the unfortunate officer.[33] If Buckingham intended a satire on Monmouth, it would have been easy to combine the characters of Pretty-man and Drawcansir to produce a painfully recognizable portrait. Sir William Coventry had fallen from power in 1669, as a direct result of Buckingham's attack on him in *The Country Gentleman*. When *The Rehearsal* reached the stage he was in retirement, no longer a tempting target.

The evidence for the equation of Bayes with Arlington seems to be limited to the patch on the nose. Bayes's conversation is ridiculous: his manners are absurdly obsequious, he fumbles for words, he boasts of talking bawdy. Arlington, on the other hand, was smooth and diplomatic. Evelyn calls him "absolutely the best bred and Courtly person his Majestie has about him."[34] Pepys, who distrusted him, wrote in his diary, "He speaks well."[35] Whereas Mr. Bayes boasts of his sexual prowess, Arlington was untouched by scandal in a court which was rife with it. No one among all his enemies—including Buckingham—ever accused him of keeping a mistress. Evelyn remarks that he has no vice save building an expensive house.

Finally, McFadden does not supply, nor can diligent research reveal, a single explicit statement by any contemporary observer which equates Arlington with Bayes. There is no evidence that Arlington or his partisans viewed the play as an insult to him. John Evelyn, who saw the play a week after it opened, wrote in his diary, "At the R: *Society*, whence to see the *Duke of Buckinghams* ridiculous farce

& Rhapsody called the *Recital*, bouffoning all Plays yet prophane enough—I returned home."[36] The entry makes it clear that Evelyn regarded the play simply as a theatrical burlesque. And yet, as a courtier and a member of the government, he was just the kind of insider who, in McFadden's view, should have recognized that Arlington was Buckingham's real target. As a member of the Arlington faction, he would certainly have resented an insult to his friend and patron if anyone did, and if he did, he should have noted it.

The character of Mr. Bayes is funny enough without being a satire against any individual, as the continued popularity of *The Rehearsal* long after the deaths of Buckingham's contemporaries has shown. Rather than an individual, Bayes represents the creative ego—the writer's pride in what he has written, his fascination with his own ability to create imitations of life, and his exasperation with the inability of others to appreciate his creations as he thinks they should. In one of the most perceptive pieces of critical commentary ever written on this play, Sheridan Baker has said, "The quintessential fact of comedy is human ineptitude mistaking itself for omnipotence. Authorship, by nature, assumes an omnipotence it must disguise. And Bayes is authorship laid comically bare, and never more thoroughly and comically so."[37]

The Rehearsal is Buckingham's masterpiece and the basis of his fame because, like all the great burlesque works of the Restoration and eighteenth century, it compels us to laugh at something in ourselves. Having enjoyed the sentiments and the heroics of serious drama, believing momentarily in an exalted idea of our own capacity for feeling and action, we are led in *The Rehearsal* to laugh at our thinking so highly of ourselves. Even the illusions of the stage itself, which as playgoers we must enjoy, are exposed as illusions, for this play is in rehearsal, interrupted by directions and comment, where dead men get up and walk off the stage, and where we hear of Pallas's lance being filled with wine before we are shown the miracle of the wine pouring out of it. The wild imagination and energy of Mr. Bayes attract us because they resemble our own most imaginative impulses. Like Bayes, we love to imagine what can never exist. We may almost prefer, as Bayes does, the products of our imaginations to the more prosaic productions of nature. But Smith and Johnson remind us of the standards of reason and nature by which we must judge Bayes—and the Bayes in ourselves—a fool. Thus the play is finally a satire on us—on our imaginations and our willingness to believe the absurd things which those imaginations present to us.

When Dryden wrote, "I knew the author sat to himself when he drew the picture, and was the very Bayes of his own farce," he told half the truth. In Bayes Buckingham presents his own intense fertility of imagination, his own lack of restraint. But there is something of Buckingham in Smith and Johnson, too—Buckingham the ironic spectator, the epigrammatic commentator on the passing scene. Dramatizing these warring impulses in himself, Buckingham universalized them. Each of us is, in a sense, the central figure in the pageant of his own life and, in another sense, an observer on its periphery. By provoking our laughing recognition of this duality in our experience, Buckingham achieved the greatest success of his life.

Chapter Five

Buckingham's Reputation and Influence

In the Restoration and eighteenth century, the reputations of members of the nobility who aspired to literary honors often had a fate directly contrary to those of ordinary writers. Whereas an ordinary writer labored in obscurity and achieved fame, if he did so at all, only after his death, a noble author often found his slightest effusions greeted with appreciation and recognition. But after his death, as his ability to reward his admirers evaporated, his work faded from view until he was simply another name in a miscellany. Buckingham's reputation and influence were founded on genuine merit, not simply on his power and wealth, but even so, his literary reputation has undergone vicissitudes just as those of other noble authors have. He was a popular playwright in his own lifetime, but his influence then was primarily personal and political, rather than literary. During the century following his death, the popularity of his work grew as his personal and political influence disappeared. Now, however, there seems to be a reversal of the eighteenth-century situation. Except for *The Rehearsal*, Buckingham's work is nearly unknown, but his personality has once again become an object of fascination for the twentieth century.

Buckingham's Contemporary Influence

Buckingham and Shadwell. Thomas Shadwell's adaptation of Shakespeare's *Timon of Athens*, first performed in January 1678, was published with a dedication to Buckingham, thanking the duke profusely for his patronage.[1] Some modern scholars have argued that the character of Alcibiades, the libertine hero in Shadwell's version of the play, is a dramatic portrait of Buckingham. One, Alan S. Fisher, believes that Shadwell's play embodies the aesthetic, political, and moral principles which Shadwell absorbed from Buckingham—a kind of confident, literal-minded belief in the self and in the "reasonable" to which Fisher gives the name "whiggery."[2]

Certainly Buckingham and Shadwell shared many political principles. Both were adherents of the Country party, which became the Whigs, and both opposed the succession to the throne of James, duke of York. In 1677 Buckingham attained the zenith of his personal popularity when he was sent, together with three other Whig lords, to the Tower of London.[3] Alcibiades resembles Buckingham, therefore, in being a champion of the liberties of the people.

However, there is no evidence of any close personal involvement between Shadwell and Buckingham. Shadwell dedicated plays to several noblemen, always in extravagant terms, and probably as much in the hope of patronage as in acknowledgment of it.[4] The publication of *Timon* coincided not with Buckingham's imprisonment in the Tower, but with his release after he had accepted the authority of the king and asked his pardon. And Shadwell was not, as Abraham Cowley, Thomas Sprat, Martin Clifford, and several of the Court Wits were, a member of Buckingham's coterie.[5] If Buckingham influenced Shadwell, therefore, he did so more as a politician than as a writer, and his influence was indirect rather than personal.

Buckingham and Marvell. With Andrew Marvell, however, Buckingham may have had both political and personal ties. The paths of their lives crossed repeatedly. They had in common a high esteem for Thomas, Lord Fairfax, an opposition to royal power, and a belief in the unpopular cause of religious toleration. But there is no evidence that they ever collaborated on any work, and the style of their most important works is so different as to make any real influence almost impossible to discover.

In 1648 after Francis Villiers, Buckingham's younger brother, was killed by Parliamentary soldiers in a skirmish near Surbiton Common, someone—probably Marvell—composed an elegy for him. The work is surprisingly bloodthirsty:

> Much rather [Fame] I know expects to tell
> How heavy Cromwell gnasht the earth and fell.
> Or how slow Death farre from the sight of day
> The long-deceived *Fairfax* bore away.

> He best the pompe of his owne death has showne.
> And we hereafter to his honor will
> Not write so many, but so many kill.
> Till the whole Army by just vengeance come
> To be at once his Trophee and his Tombe.
>   (ll. 13-16, 124-28)[6]

If the poem is Marvell's, its Royalist sympathies foreshadow the complexity of allegiance in his much more famous *Horatian Ode upon Cromwell's Return from Ireland*. Because Marvell was now to stay in England and seek preferment there, whereas Buckingham had returned to the safety of the Continent, Marvell probably did not write the elegy in the hope of making his acquaintance. But had Marvell met the two Villiers brothers between 1645 and 1647, when all three men were in France? Some details in the poem suggest a personal acquaintance, but because we have no information of any kind about Marvell's stay in France, we cannot be certain. They might even have met before their trips abroad, at Trinity College, Cambridge, which all three attended. Although precise dates of attendance are not available for any of the three, Marvell seems to have left the college by September 1641, just about the time that the two Villiers brothers were enrolled. Still, they must have had many mutual friends there, particularly Abraham Cowley, Buckingham's lifelong friend, who may have written a part for Marvell into his undergraduate farce, *Naufragium Joculare*, and whose poem appeared with Marvell's in the miscellany, *Musa Cantabrigis* (1637).[7]

In 1651, after General Fairfax had resigned his command, Marvell was brought to Nun Appleton to become tutor to Fairfax's daughter, Mary, who was to marry the duke of Buckingham in 1657. Marvell left Fairfax's employ in 1652 to become tutor to William Dutton, a scholar at Eton. By 1657 he was Latin secretary to Cromwell, the Lord Protector. He could not, therefore, have met Buckingham at Nun Appleton. But as we noted in chapter 2, there are some interesting similarities between Marvell's *Horatian Ode* and Buckingham's 1672 "Epitaph on Thomas, Third Lord Fairfax." If these similarities are quotations or allusions, then Buckingham must have seen the *Horatian Ode* in manuscript, for it was not published until 1681.

In 1659, Marvell was elected to Parliament representing the city of Hull, his birthplace, and he continued to serve in the House of

Commons until his death in 1678. Although he supported the king and Lord Chancellor Clarendon's admininstration immediately after the Restoration, by about 1665 he began to oppose Clarendon, and in doing so he became informally allied with Buckingham, who had opposed Clarendon personally and politically since the Interregnum. For the remainder of his life Marvell was usually opposed to the policies of whatever ministry was in power. Therefore he was theoretically on opposite sides from Buckingham during the period from 1667 to 1674 when Buckingham was chief minister of the Cabal, but on the same side after 1674, when Buckingham himself was active in opposition.

Marvell's letters to friends and supporters in Hull contain repeated references to Buckingham. The earlier references are often items of scandal: Buckingham's being challenged to a duel by the earl of Sandwich, his being committed to the Tower of London for scuffling with the marquess of Dorchester, and his running into debt. Reporting Buckingham's affair with the countess of Shrewsbury (and, by implication, his neglect of Marvell's former pupil, Mary Fairfax Villiers, the duchess of Buckingham), Marvell speaks with dry irony: "*Buckingham* runs out of all with the *Lady Shrewsbury,* by whom he believes he had a Son, to whom the King stood Godfather...." But after Buckingham enters the opposition, Marvell speaks more sympathetically of him. He informs his constituents of Buckingham's confinement to the Tower in 1677 and even cheers the famous Buckingham wit when it is employed on the side of religious toleration: "Never were poor Men exposed and abused, all the Session, as the Bishops were by the *Duke of Buckingham,* upon the Test; never the like, nor so infinitely pleasant: and no Men were ever grown so odiously ridiculous."[8]

During these years Marvell wrote a series of biting verse satires against the ministry and its conduct of public affairs. Given their length and breadth and Marvell's well-known antipathy to the morals of the courtiers, it is somewhat surprising that Buckingham, who was chief minister during the first part of the period, is never attacked in them. Could Marvell have refrained from attacking the duke because of a personal friendship, perhaps a secret friendship, between them? Christopher Wase, in his poem "Divination" (1666), accuses Buckingham of being the secret author of the "Second Advice to a Painter," a poem almost universally believed to be the work of Marvell. Could Wase have known of an otherwise undiscovered collaboration between the two poet-politicans? A recent editor acknowledges that the possibility cannot be ruled out.[9] The anonymous "Litany of the Duke of Buckingham" accuses Buckingham of deserting old friends for "Wildman and Marvell." An entry in the *Calendar of State Papers* seems to imply that Buckingham, Marvell, and the mysterious Colonel Thomas Blood were involved together in some espionage against the French in 1671.[10]

It is fascinating to imagine that Marvell and Buckingham might have worked in concert as secret agents for Charles as early as the 1650s. Such a hypothesis would account for Marvell's ability to save Milton, his predecessor as Cromwell's Latin secretary, from prosecution after the Restoration, and possibly for Buckingham's entrée to the Fairfax family in 1657. But there is no conclusive evidence for such speculation. Even if it were true, we probably could not discover today what both men endeavored to conceal in the 1660s and 1670s.

In 1672, Marvell publicly entered the controversy over religious toleration by writing a prose pamphlet entitled *The Rehearsal Transpros'd*. The pamphlet took its name from the exchange between Bayes, Smith, and Johnson in Buckingham's *The Rehearsal*, act 1, when Bayes speaks of his "Rule of Transversion, or *Regula Duplex*: changing Verse into Prose, or Prose into verse, *alternative* as you please," and Johnson replies, "Methinks, Mr. *Bayes*, that putting Verse into prose should be call'd Transprosing" (1. 1. 96–98, 106–7). In addition to the title, Marvell took the name "Bayes" from the central character in Buckingham's farce and applied it to his antagonist, Dr. Samuel Parker. He also compares Parker to Amaryllis and to Drawcansir. In addition, he mentions in passing John Lacy, who played Bayes in the 1671 production; Mr. Cartwright, who played Thunder; the Usher-King and the Physician-King; and Smith and Johnson.[11] Despite all these references to *The Rehearsal*, however, *The Rehearsal Transpros'd* does not really show the literary influence of Buckingham's farce. It is a work of political controversy. It does not have the two-part structure of *The Rehearsal*, nor the dramatic form, nor the critical concerns. For Marvell Bayes is what some critics and scholars have mistakenly thought he was for Buckingham: a caricature of an enemy and no more.

Thus although Marvell and Buckingham may indeed have been political allies, their modes of writing were essentially very different. Buckingham, primarily a dramatist, used a genre completely foreign to Marvell, and Marvell's greatest poems are so private that they were almost certainly unknown in his lifetime. Although the possibility of the two men's being secret friends and co-conspirators remains teasingly alive, there is no conclusive evidence to support it.

Hostile portraits of Buckingham. Buckingham was prominent and controversial in English politics at a time when political controversy often found its way into literature. It is not surprising, therefore, that he was the subject of many satirical attacks in both prose and verse.

The most famous of these attacks is Dryden's portrait of Zimri in *Absalom and Achitophel*. Among the others are prose characters of Buckingham written by Samuel Butler and Bishop Burnet, and several verse satires by anonymous writers. The verse satires include "On the Prorogation" (1671), in which about sixty lines are devoted to Buckingham; another verse satire beginning "I sing the praise of a worthy wight" and appearing under various titles in ten different manuscripts; and one entitled "A Litany of the Duke of Buckingham," apparently written in 1680.[12]

The motives of Dryden, Burnet, and the anonymous verse satirists in attacking Buckingham are easy enough to understand. All of them were opposed to Buckingham politically, and Burnet genuinely, rather than simply rhetorically, disapproved of Buckingham's morals. But why Samuel Butler, whom Buckingham employed as his secretary during his missions to France and Holland in the early 1670s and with whom he collaborated on *The Rehearsal*, might have turned on his patron is a question for which there is now no ready answer.

The art of the lampooner is to make a caricature of his victim. However, in the most memorable cases the caricature is the creation not of a single poet but of a group of satirists, each satirist accepting the portrait from his predecessors, refining out of it the incidental details, and passing on an intensified version to the next. By this method a kind of communal myth was created, one which could replace the real man in the mind of the community. Indeed, the myth could affect the reality, so that the man might find himself in some magical way forced to become the myth. By surveying the satires on Buckingham, we can understand how Dryden's art enriched and transformed the myth and finally fixed it permanently in the public mind.[13]

The most frequent and detailed charges against Buckingham are those of sexual deviance. Almost no satirist fails to mention the famous affair with the countess of Shrewsbury, and most join to that charge the accusation of murder for Buckingham's killing the earl in the duel at Barn Elms in 1668. In addition he is accused of incest with his sister, the duchess of Richmond ("I sing the praise," ll. 12, 15), of homosexuality with the actor Edward Kynaston ("I sing the praise," ll. 19–20; "Litany," ll. 12, 15), and of impotence ("Litany," l. 48). Butler's prose character, without making specific charges, makes the general charge most sinister:

> A Duke of Bucks is one that has studied the whole Body of Vice.... His Appetite to his Pleasures is diseased and crazy.... Perpetual Surfeits of Pleasure have filled his Mind with bad and vicious Humours (as well as his Body with a Nursery of Diseases) which makes him affect new and extravagant Ways, as being sick and tired with the Old.... And as the same Dose of the same Physic has no Operation on those, that are much used to it; so his Pleasures require a larger Proportion of Excess and Variety, to render him sensible of them.

Dryden, who, in his own words, "avoided the mention of great crimes," glances at Buckingham's sexual reputation only in his use of the name "Zimri" (see chapter 2).

Another charge against Buckingham, certainly a just one, is that of profligacy with his money. The "Litany" notes his

> being still cheated by th' same undertakers,
> By Levellers, bawds, saints, chemists and Quakers,
> Who make us gold-finders and themselves gold-makers.
> (ll. 28–30)

"Gold-finder" is a slang term for a cleaner of privies. Burnet, too, says that "he was drawn into chemistry, and for years he thought he was very near the finding the philosopher's stone; which had the fate that attends on all such men as he was, when they are drawn in, to lay out for it." But once again Dryden makes the charge most tellingly:

> In squandring Wealth was his peculiar Art:
> Nothing went unrewarded, but Desert.
> Begger'd by Fools, whom still he found too late:
> He had his Jest, and they had his Estate.
> (ll. 559–62)

Buckingham's talent for mimicry, applied to the king, seemed to hostile commentators an act of disloyalty. Burnet writes, "He was bred about the king, and for many years he had a great ascendant over him: but he spake of him to all persons with that contempt that at last he drew a lasting disgrace upon himself," and the "Litany" speaks of his "mimical acting all those above us." From this kind of disloyalty treachery is only a short step away. "On the Prorogation" speaks of Buckingham's treachery in abandoning the king in France in 1657 to come to England to wed Mary Fairfax. And the "Litany" accuses him of plotting to overthrow both the king and Parliament and set up a commonwealth with himself at its head. For Dryden, of course, the charge of disloyalty needed no special emphasis, since Zimri appears at the head of the catalog of rebels in *Absalom and Achitophel*.

A frequent charge is that of inconstancy. Burnet wrote, "He had no principles either of religion, virtue, or friendship.... He was true to nothing: for he was not true to himself." Butler wrote, "He is as inconstant as the Moon, which he lives under." "On the Prorogation" applies this charge to Buckingham's politics: "He all things is, but unto nothing true, / All old things hates, but can abide no new" (ll. 88–89). In Dryden's portrait of Buckingham, the charge of inconstancy becomes the principle of his character. As Dryden sees him, Buckingham

> Was every thing by starts, and nothing long:
> But in the course of one revolving Moon,
> Was Chymist, Fidler, States-Man, and Buffoon:
> Then all for Women, Painting, Rhiming, Drinking;
> Besides ten thousand freaks that dy'd in thinking.
> Blest Madman, who coud every hour employ,
> With something New to wish, or to enjoy!
> (ll. 548–54)

Buckingham was a chemist: like King Charles, he was interested in chemistry and had his own laboratory. Like Dryden himself, Buckingham was a Fellow of the Royal Society. Like Samuel Pepys, Buckingham was a musician, who composed and performed on the violin. But when a violinist is called a "fiddler," or when his writing poetry is called "rhyming," or when an actor is called a "buffoon," these pursuits are made to seem foolish and trivial. And when they are put together in a series, they reflect on one another. The reader senses, from the juxtaposition of "chymist" and "fiddler," that when Buckingham was doing chemical experiments he was only "fiddling around," and from the juxtaposition of "statesman" and "buffoon" that when he acted as a statesman he was only a buffoon. Thus the ability to do many things well which we ordinarily associate with the "Renaissance man" becomes in this portrait an indication of the reckless, unbounded, dangerous energy and feverish imagination of a "blest madman." As Jean Hagstrum has written, Zimri "is tortured out of shape by imagination.... Buckingham is various, an epitome of levity, a spinning top that draws all unstable motion to itself, the whirligig of revolutionary energy."[14] Thus Dryden's Zimri is a masterpiece, the completion of that collaboration involving tradition, satirist and—unintentionally—victim, which makes great satire. Of the several kinds of literary influence that Buckingham exerted upon his contemporaries, certainly one of the most important was his sitting for his portrait.

Buckingham's Influence in the Eighteenth Century

In the eighteenth century, as Buckingham's personal influence faded and as new political controversies supplanted those in which he had been embroiled, his personal and political importance ended, but the popularity of his dramatic works on the stage actually increased.

The Chances in Buckingham's adaptation was frequently revived after its initial success in 1667. Although performance records before 1704 are incomplete, we know that one popular revival took place in 1690–91 and that there had been others earlier. In the eighteenth century Buckingham's version became a stock play in the repertoire of the dramatic companies. In November of 1754, for example, it was performed eight times. The role of Don John, first played by Charles Hart in 1667, was later taken by such popular actors as Wilks and Garrick. That of the Second Constantia, probably created by Nell Gwynn, was also performed by Charlotte Butler, Anne Oldfield, and several others. There were six editions of *The Chances* before 1800.

The Rehearsal was even more popular. It went through five separate quarto editions, each with revisions and additions, before Buckingham's death, and twelve editions were published in the eighteenth century. Although we have records of only six performances before

1700, *The Rehearsal* was performed literally hundreds of times in the eighteenth century. Its success on the stage reached a peak in the 1740s, when there were ninety-two performances, and then fell off gradually into the 1770s, when its popularity finally dwindled more than a century after its debut. The role of Bayes became a vehicle for many of the greatest comic actors of the period. After John Lacy, who played Bayes in the first two performances, the part was taken by Richard Estcourt, then by Colley Cibber, by Theophilus Cibber, and by David Garrick. Such lesser performers as Samuel Foote, James Dance, and even the actress Catherine Clive, also appeared occasionally in the role. Garrick, the greatest Bayes, played the role eighty-eight times in his career, and it was Garrick's retirement in 1776 which led to the disappearance of *The Rehearsal* from the dramatic repertoire.[15]

Because of its popular success, *The Rehearsal* helped to build and shape the tradition of burlesque drama, which may be the eighteenth century's most vital contribution to the literature of the theater. Buckingham did not, of course, invent theatrical burlesque. Nor did he invent the "rehearsal play," in which we see the inner drama being rehearsed. Earlier rehearsal plays in English include Shakespeare's *Midsummer Night's Dream* (1595) and Davenant's *The Play-house to Be Let* (1663), and Buckingham may also have drawn upon Moliere's *Impromptu de Versailles* (1663).[16] But Buckingham did influence the directions which the tradition took in the eighteenth century.

Eighteenth-century burlesque theater developed a dynamic tradition. Each playwright drew on the work of his predecessors, on his own imagination, and on the contemporary serious stage for ideas. Buckingham's influence was sometimes explicitly acknowledged: Fielding's *The Author's Farce* (1730) mentions Drawcansir and Parthenope in its prologue and the kings of Brentford in its final act, and the prologue to Sheridan's *The Critic* (1779) speaks of "Those gay days of wickedness and wit, / When Villiers criticiz'd what Dryden writ."[17] But writers only occasionally paid homage to their models; for the most part they simply made the tradition their property and were content to use it, modify it, and enrich it—just as Buckingham himself had done in *The Rehearsal*.

For example, in *The Rehearsal*, act 2, scene 1, we have the following exchange:

Physician. Sir, to conclude.
Smith. What, before he begins?
Bayes. No, Sir; you must know, they had been talking of this a pretty while without.
Smith. Where? in the Tyring-room?
Bayes. Why, ay, Sir. He's so dull!

Buckingham's joke here is a fundamental one in theatrical burlesque. Bayes is unable to recognize the distinction between the make-believe world of the stage and the real one of the dressing room. This playing with a necessary convention of the theater naturally attracted imitation. Fielding, in *Pasquin* (1736), adapts Buckingham's idea:

Miss Mayoress. Ha! and can you be so generous to forgive all my ill-usage of you?
Fustian. What ill-usage, Mr. Trapwit? For if I mistake not, this is the first time these lovers spoke to one another.
Trapwit. What ill-usage, sir? A great deal, sir.
Fustian. When, sir? Where, sir?
Trapwit. Why, behind the scenes, sir. What, would you have every thing brought upon the stage? (3. 1.)[18]

In Sheridan's *The Critic*, the inner play opens with another interrupted conversation:

[*Enter* Sir Walter Raleigh *and* Sir Christopher Hatton.]
Sir Christopher. "True, gallant Raleigh!"
Dangle. What, they had been talking before?
Puff. O, yes; all the way as they came along. (2. 1)

The same idea was thus used successfully three separate times by three first-rate comic writers. Each recognized the comic value of the joke, and each made it his own. Dane Farnsworth Smith lists some sixty-five burlesque plays written and performed between the debut of *The Rehearsal* and the Licensing Act of 1737. We can assume that Buckingham's great farce is one of the principle sources of the tradition in which these plays were written, even when no direct imitation is apparent.

Among the plays which take part in the tradition are such famous examples as Gay's *The What d'Ye Call It* (1715) and *The Beggar's Opera* (1728) and Fielding's *The Author's Farce* (1730), *The Tragedy of Tragedies, or the Life and Death of Tom Thumb the Great* (1730), and *Pasquin* (1736). None of the many plays in the tradition, however, shows Buckingham's influence more clearly than Sheridan's *The Critic*—nor is there any play which, despite its debt to the tradition, is more original. Sheridan in effect divides the character of Bayes in two, presenting two foolish playwrights. One of them, Sir Fretful Plagiary, has Bayes's vanity, his false humility, and his tendency to plagiarism. The other, Puff, an admitted hack, is the author of the inner play which we see. Sheridan also shortens the action of the whole play from five acts to three, a change for which audiences can be grateful, for nonsense ceases to be amusing when it goes on too long.

The number of Sheridan's borrowings from Buckingham is large, but almost everything that is borrowed is in some way transformed. For example, whereas Bayes enunciates as a general rule "You must ever make a *simile*, when you are surpris'd; 'tis the new way of writing" (2. 3. 15–17), Puff leans to piety as an all-purpose tool: "In great emergencies, there is nothing like a prayer" (2. 1). Whereas Bayes makes the two rightful kings of Brentford overhear the plotting whispers of the Physician and Gentleman-Usher (2. 2. 46–51), Puff makes the two ostensibly sleeping sentinels overhear the conversation between Sir Christopher Hatton, Sir Walter Raleigh, the earl of Leicester, and their companions (2. 1). Bayes has the two usurper-kings prepare to commit suicide in grief for the death of Lardella, then transforms the scene into one of rejoicing at a word from Pallas: "Hold, stop your murd'ring hands / At Pallases commands" (4. 1. 179–80). Puff presents a scene in which the two nieces threaten Whiskerandos with daggers, their two uncles threaten him with swords, and Whiskerandos threatens to stab the two nieces with daggers; then he has them all drop their weapons when the Beefeater enters and commands, "In the Queen's name I charge you all to drop / Your swords and daggers!" (3. 1). As Bayes precipitates his grand battle by having the Lieutenant General "give the lie" to the General (5. 1. 216), Puff starts the duel between Whiskerandos and the Beefeater in the same way (3. 1). The scene in which Prince Pretty-man worries over whether he is or is not the son of a fisherman (3. 4) is matched in Puff's play by the recognition scene in which

Tom Jenkens discovers that he is not the son of a fishmonger (3. 1). Even Lardella's transmigration to the body of a "humble-bee" (4. 1. 144) is glanced at in Tilburina's "mad scene," in the lines, "Is this a grasshopper!—Ha! no, it is my / Whiskerandos" (3. 1).[19]

The heroic couplet drama which *The Rehearsal* had mocked had departed from the serious stage by Sheridan's time, but the "age of prose and sense" which Buckingham had hoped for in his epilogue had not succeeded it. In place of the overblown heroics of the Restoration, the later eighteenth century loved the noble and the sentimental, usually written in blank verse and often in an imitation of Elizabethan diction. Puff's play, therefore, is written entirely in blank verse, and there are hilariously blatant plagiarisms of Shakespeare, as when the Beefeater opens his soliloquy with "Perdition catch my soul, but I do love thee" (compare *Othello*, 3. 3. 90–91).

Sheridan follows Buckingham, as Gay had done in *The Beggar's Opera*, in burying political innuendo in his dramatic burlesque, but whereas Buckingham, a member of the ministry himself, had attacked only individual political figures, Sheridan indicts the general conduct of affairs. In 1779 England was at war against its American colonies, which had declared their independence, and against France and Spain, which had combined forces to send an invasion fleet against England. The ministry of Lord North seemed unable to summon the resolution to oppose its enemies effectively. Thus the subject of Puff's play, *The Spanish Armada*, is particularly timely, and the depiction of Lord Burleigh, Queen Elizabeth's chief minister, as too preoccupied with state affairs to speak (3. 1), was easily seen as a reference to Lord North.[20] But these political analogues are made more explicit by the references to contemporary affairs in the conversation between Mr. and Mrs. Dangle in act 1. The ridicule of patriotic rhetoric which Sheridan began in *The Critic* (see, for example, act 2, scene 1 and act 3, scene 1) became a permanent feature of English burlesque drama.[21]

Thus *The Critic* completed the process of the assimilation of Buckingham's influence into the tradition of the burlesque theatre. After 1779 *The Rehearsal* ceased almost completely to be performed on the stage.

Buckingham in the Twentieth Century

Like Buckingham's contemporaries, we in the twentieth century are more interested in him as a personality than as a literary figure.

Since the eighteenth century his literary works have lost most of their popularity, but interest in his life—and in his writings as expressive of his mind—has increased. Neither *The Rehearsal* nor Buckingham's revision of *The Chances* is known on the twentieth-century stage. Although the burlesque theater continues to be as strong and lively as it was in the eighteenth century, authors derive their ideas and inspiration from their more immediate predecessors and from Buckingham only insofar as he is a part of a broader tradition. In the twentieth century other burlesque dramas of the Augustan age have been frequently revived: Sheridan's *The Critic* has been produced at least five times since 1900, and Gay's *Beggar's Opera* many more times than that, in addition to being revised by Weill and Brecht as the *Threepenny Opera*. But *The Rehearsal*, the ancestor of these, has been presented only once, in 1952, in a two-act New York performance whose resounding failure must surely have discouraged any further attempts at production.[22]

On the other hand, Buckingham's life and character have come to fascinate us. Three times in the twentieth century he has been the subject of biographies—each with a more provocative title than its predecessor. We find Buckingham so fascinating, no doubt, because we recognize in his character something akin to ourselves, something which we do not see in some of his better-known contemporaries.

Toward the most cherished artistic and social values of his time, Buckingham held ambivalent attitudes—sometimes admiring them or striving to achieve them, sometimes mocking or subverting them. His slavish adherence to a narrow decorum vitiates his revision of Beaumont's and Fletcher's *Philaster*, yet his inspired manipulation of decorum gives life and truth to his elegy for Fairfax. Even in a time when no act of state could take place without its measure of pomp, Buckingham's love of costume and ceremony was unusual; for example, the procession to celebrate his installation as chancellor of Cambridge in 1671 was almost royally elaborate. Yet it was Buckingham who saw through the empty pretentions of his contemporaries, he who mocked the solemnity of Clarendon and Arlington, he who recognized the value of plainness in Fairfax. These contradictions make him difficult to categorize, but today we know that unrecognized contradictions are part of all human nature.

When Dryden wrote of *The Rehearsal*, "I knew the author sat to himself when he drew the picture, and was the very Bayes of his own farce," he recognized Buckingham's powerful affinity for the unrestrained imagination which Bayes represents. Like the speaker in Swift's *A Tale of a Tub*, Bayes fascinates us because we see in his egotistical, illogical, ultimately insane view of the world something of the creative imagination of his creator—and to a lesser degree, something of ourselves as well. The tug of war between Bayes, Smith, and Johnson in the outer play of *The Rehearsal* represents that struggle between the fancy and the judgment which takes place whenever we write and whenever we read.

In Buckingham's greatest work and in the most flamboyant actions of his life, he is one representative, though not the most distinguished one, of the strain of seventeenth-century thought most like our own: hyperbolic rather than restrained, various rather than orderly, intensely energetic rather than coolly detached, seeking rather than knowing. Like Donne, Rochester, and Swift, and unlike Dryden, Addison, and Pope, Buckingham saw in disorder not the antithesis of art but the materials of art. The enormous energy, the rapid shifts of focus, the inability to accept limits—all the qualities in him which fascinated and shocked his friends as well as his enemies, and which bewildered even Buckingham himself—these are qualities which we in the twentieth century comprehend no more fully than Buckingham's contemporaries did but which we recognize in ourselves more readily than they. The vitality and variety which the elegance of Charles's court could not repress are still, after three centuries, very much alive and as appealing as ever. "It was difficult to do without him," wrote Grammont, "when he had a mind to make himself agreeable." Once we have made his acquaintance, we often find that it still is.

Notes and References

Chapter One

1. Winifred Burghclere, *George Villiers, Second Duke of Buckingham, 1628–1687: A Study in the History of the Restoration* (London, 1903), pp. 220–21.
2. Samuel Johnson, "Life of Cowley," in *Lives of the English Poets*, 2 vols. (New York: Dutton, 1964), 1:11.
3. Joseph Spence, *Anecdotes, Observations, and Characters of Books and Men* (London, 1820), p. 63.
4. Anthony Hamilton, *The Memoirs of Count Grammont*, ed. Gordon Goodwin, 2 vols. (Edinburgh, 1908), 1:137; Gilbert Burnet, *History of My Own Time*, ed. Osmund Airy, 2 vols. (Oxford, 1897–1900), 1:89–90.
5. Quoted in Hester W. Chapman, *Great Villiers: A Study of George Villiers Second Duke of Buckingham, 1628–1687* (London, 1949), p. 53.
6. *Archives des Affaires Etrangers*, no. 135 f. 40, (13 July 1679), quoted in Burghclere, *George Villiers*, p. 367.
7. Chapman, *Great Villiers*, p. 92.
8. Fairfax Papers (British Library MSS Harl. 6862–6896), 4:253, quoted in Burghclere, *George Villiers*, p. 96.
9. Burnet, *History of My Own Time*, 1:295.
10. It was treason to cast the king's horoscope because the horoscope would predict the exact day and hour of his death. See John Harold Wilson, *A Rake and His Times: George Villiers, Second Duke of Buckingham* (New York, 1954), p. 77.
11. Samuel Pepys, *The Diary of Samuel Pepys*, ed. Robert Latham and William Matthews, 11 vols. (Berkeley, 1970–83), 8:79.
12. Ibid., 9:208.
13. Ibid., 8:535.
14. David Ogg, *England in the Reign of Charles II*, 2 vols. (Oxford, 1934), 1:344–46.
15. He had been wounded at the Battle of Andover, in 1644, fighting for the Royalists in the Civil War. See Violet Barbour, *Henry Bennet Earl of Arlington, Secretary of State to Charles II* (Washington, 1914), pp. 46–47.
16. John Dryden, *Absalom and Achitophel*, ll. 534–568, in *The*

Works of John Dryden, ed. H. T. Swedenberg and Vinton A. Dearing, 20 vols. (Berkeley, 1956–), 2:21–22.

    17. Laurence Echard, *The History of England,* 3 vols. (London, 1707–18), 3:842.

    18. Burnet, *History of My Own Time,* 1:182. See also the *Memoirs of Count Grammont,* 1:137: "His particular talent consisted in turning into ridicule whatever was ridiculous in other people, and in taking them off, even in their presence, without their perceiving it."

Chapter Two

    1. The duke of Buckingham's commonplace book is in the possession of the earl of Jersey; quotations from it are used with his permission. Selections from the book have been published in the *Quarterly Review* 187 (1898):86–112, and in the three biographies of Buckingham published by Burghclere, Chapman, and Wilson. I have normalized the spelling, punctuation, and other accidentals of poems quoted from the commonplace book in this chapter.

    2. *Princeton Encyclopedia of Poetry and Poetics,* ed. Alex Preminger, Frank J. Warnke, and O. B. Hardison, Jr. (Princeton, 1965), p. 247.

    3. See Hoyt H. Hudson, *The Epigram in the English Renaissance* (New York, 1966).

    4. Gotthold Ephraim Lessing, *Fables and Epigrams: with Essays on Fable and Epigram,* trans. J. and H. L. Hunt (London, 1825).

    5. Pierre Nicole, *An Essay on True and Apparent Beauty in which from Settled Principles Is Rendered the Grounds for Choosing and Rejecting Epigrams* (Paris, 1659), trans. J. V. Cunningham, Augustan Reprint Society, no. 24 (Los Angeles, 1950), pp. 16–17.

    6. *John Donne's Poetry,* ed. A. L. Clements (New York, 1966), p. 38.

    7. Dryden, *Absalom and Achitophel,* ll. 355–56. For the full context, see chapter 1, above.

    8. Robert C. Elliott, *The Power of Satire: Magic, Ritual, Art* (Princeton, 1960), pp. 3–48.

    9. The attempt on Buckingham's life was made by Abraham Goodman, a servant, in 1663. See Wilson, *A Rake and His Times,* p. 23.

    10. This poem is almost certainly aimed at Heneage Finch (1621–82), who was lord chancellor of England from 1675 until his death, rather than at Edward Hyde, earl of Clarendon (1609–74), who was lord chancellor from 1660–1667. The practices ascribed to the subject are completely out of character for Clarendon, who was known for his formal dignity and gravity, and the neighborhood mentioned in the poem

fits Finch, who lived in Lincoln's Inn Fields, but not Clarendon, whose house was in St. James's Street, Picadilly.
   11. Arthur O. Lovejoy, *The Great Chain of Being: A Study in the History of an Idea* (New York, 1960). "Plant animals," mentioned in line 2, are zoophytes such as coral or sponges.
   12. Burghclere, *George Villiers*, p. 113.
   13. No printed edition of this poem appeared in Buckingham's lifetime. In *A Third Collection of...Poems, Satires, Songs, &c. against Popery and Tyranny* (1689), the first published edition, the poem is entitled "An Epitaph on Thomas, third Lord Fairfax." In Buckingham's *Miscellaneous Works*, 1704, and subsequent editions, it carries the title, "A Pindaric Poem on the Death of the Lord Fairfax, Father to the Duchess Dowager of Buckingham." The term "Pindaric" was loosely used in the Restoration for any ode except the Horatian. See William F. Thrall, Addison Hibbard, and C. Hugh Holman, *A Handbook to Literature* (New York, 1960), pp. 327–28.
   No reliable edition of Buckingham's nondramatic works is readily available. Unless otherwise specified, quotations in this chapter from Buckingham's published poems are taken from *The Genuine Works of His Grace George Villiers, Duke of Buckingham* (Glasgow, 1752).
   14. "Braves" are "bravoes"—bullies or hired assassins. A "pudder" (or "pother") is a commotion or fuss. The first word is street slang, the second homely and conversational. "Polls" may be Buckingham's own coinage; it means "hack politicians."
   15. William R. Orwen, in "Marvell and Buckingham," *Notes and Queries* 196 (1951):10–11, suggests that Buckingham's ode echoes words and phrases in Marvell's *Horatian Ode Upon Cromwell's Return from Ireland* (1650) in order to heighten the contrast between Fairfax and Cromwell. On possible relations between Buckingham and Marvell, see chapter 5, below.
   16. An epithalamion is a poem in celebration of a marriage; it is a separate genre from the love lyric. But Buckingham's epithalamion has enough in common with his love poems to make it worthwhile to consider them together.
   17. Aurora and Tithonus appear in lines 74–76, Hesperus in line 95, of Spenser's poem.
   18. See John Harold Wilson, *Court Satires of the Restoration* (Columbus, 1976), and my own "Sexuality, Deviance, and Moral Character in the Personal Satire of the Restoration," *Eighteenth-Century Life* 2 (1975):16–19.
   19. "A Familiar Epistle to Mr. Julian," like all the published poems in this chapter, is quoted from the 1752 edition of Buckingham's works. However, there is an edition of the poem in the *Poems on Affairs of*

State, 7 vols., ed. George deF. Lord (New Haven, 1963), 1:387–91, with full commentary and footnotes.

20. The ivory staff is the symbol of high office carried by several of the king's ministers. "Tatta" is Arlington's daughter Isabella, who was born in 1667.

21. "The Works of George Villiers, Duke of Buckingham," ed. Thomas Percy, 2 vols. (1809), 1:165. In the absence of a readily available edition of Buckingham's miscellaneous prose, I have relied whenever necessary on this authoritative but unpublished edition. There is a copy in the British Library.

22. A reply to it (*A Short Answer to His Grace the Duke of Buckingham's Paper*) and Buckingham's brief reply to the reply (*The Duke of Buckingham his Grace's Letter to the Unknown Author*) make oblique references to King James's pledge, made to Parliament in May 1685, to uphold the constitution and the Church of England. See David Ogg, *England in the Reigns of James II and William III* (Oxford, 1955), p. 143.

23. *Two Speeches* (Amsterdam, 1675), p. 12.

24. "So potent was religion in persuading to evil deeds" (*De Rerum Natura* [*On the Nature of Things*], bk. 1, l. 101).

25. "Works of Buckingham," ed. Percy, 2:177–78.

26. On Buckingham's reputation, see Wilson, *A Rake and His Times*, pp. 218–19.

27. See Stanley Fish, *Self-Consuming Artifacts: The Experience of Seventeenth-Century Literature* (Berkeley, 1972), particularly pp. 400–401.

28. *A Short Discourse upon the Reasonableness of Men's Having a Religion, or Worship of God* (London, 1685).

29. Of course, critics may argue that the illogic in the *Short Discourse* is inadvertent. To support that view, however, these critics must be prepared to explain why Buckingham, eleven years after renouncing, in the letter to Martin Clifford, the use of reason to persuade the public of religious truth, would set out to write a genuinely logical treatise on religion.

30. See John Harold Wilson, *The Court Wits of the Restoration: An Introduction* (Princeton, 1948).

Chapter Three

1. All references to Buckingham's version of *The Chances* in this chapter are to *The Chances, A Comedy: As It Was Acted at the Theater Royal. Corrected and Altered by a Person of Honour.* (London, 1682).

2. References in this chapter to Fletcher's version of *The Chances*

Notes and References 131

are to the edition by George Walton Williams in *The Dramatic Works in the Beaumont and Fletcher Canon*, ed. Fredson Bowers, 4 vols. (Cambridge, 1966–79), 4:541–645.

3. Dryden, "Defense of the Epilogue: or, an Essay on the Dramatic Poetry of the Last Age," in *Of Dramatic Poesy and Other Critical Essays*, ed. George Watson, 2 vols. (New York, 1962), 1:180.

4. Arthur Colby Sprague, *Beaumont and Fletcher on the Restoration Stage* (Cambridge, Mass., 1926), p. 223.

5. Sir Robert Howard and George Villiers, *The Country Gentleman: A "Lost" Play and Its Background*, ed. Arthur H. Scouten and Robert D. Hume (Philadelphia, 1976). All quotations from *The Country Gentleman* in this chapter are taken from this edition.

6. Pepys, *Diary*, 9:225.

7. Ibid., pp. 471–72. On the night of 31 January of the same year, Edward Kynaston, an actor who had played the part of Sir Charles Sedley in the play *The Heiress*, was assaulted in St. James's Park by hired thugs and severely beaten.

8. Ibid., pp. 467–68.

9. Burghclere, *George Villiers*, p. 209.

10. *Country Gentleman*, p. 26.

11. *Bonne mine:* literally, "good air," elegant manner.

12. *Country Gentleman*, p. 30.

13. Ibid., p. 89.

14. See John Harrington Smith, *The Gay Couple in Restoration Comedy* (Cambridge, 1948), pp. 77–78.

15. Howard's attack on the unities appeared in his preface to his last performed play, *The Duke of Lerma* (1668). See *Country Gentleman*, p. 21.

16. See Howard's *The Committee* (1662) and Buckingham's *The Chances*. On the appearance of this formula in Restoration comedy, see Robert D. Hume, *The Development of English Drama in the Late Seventeenth Century* (Oxford, 1976), pp. 130–31.

17. The revision was accepted as Buckingham's work by Bishop Percy in his unpublished late eighteenth-century edition, by A. C. Sprague in *Beaumont and Fletcher on the Restoration Stage*, and by Arthur Mizener in "George Villiers" (Ph.D. diss., Princeton University, 1934).

18. *Of Dramatic Poesy*, ed. Watson, 1:172.

19. Buckingham changes the names of all the characters in the play, being careful to keep the names metrically equivalent for the sake of his versification. In addition to the changes just mentioned there are these: Dion = Cleon; Pharamond = Thrasomond; Thrasilene = Agremont; Cleremont = Adelard; Megra = Alga; Galatea = Melisinda.

20. Quotations from *Philaster* are taken from the edition by Robert

K. Turner in *The Dramatic Works in the Beaumont and Fletcher Canon* (Cambridge, 1966–79), 1:367–504.

21. References to *The Restauration* are to Bishop Percy's edition of Buckingham's works, 1:229–346.

22. Ogg, *England in the Reign of Charles II*, 1:379.

23. Opinion is divided on the question of Feversham's incompetence. See Winston Churchill, *Marlborough: His Life and Times*, 6 vols. (New York, 1933), 1:217–18; and G. J. Wolseley, *The Life of John Churchill, Duke of Marlborough*, 2 vols. (London, 1894), 1:281, 307–8.

24. Wolseley, *Life of John Churchill*, 1:281. Feversham was, in fact, a French Protestant, who had exiled himself to England to avoid religious persecution in his native land.

25. *Poems on Affairs of State*, vol. 4, ed. Galbraith M. Crump (New Haven, 1968), 270. The reward to which the satirist alludes is the Order of the Garter, conferred upon Feversham on 30 July 1685 as a reward for his having defeated Monmouth.

26. References to *The Battle of Sedgmoor* are to Percy's edition of Buckingham's works, 2:39–46.

27. Grammont, *Memoirs*, 1:137.

28. As in chapter 2, all references to and quotations from the duke of Buckingham's commonplace book are by permission of the earl of Jersey.

29. Buckingham (or his source) made no attempt to be faithful to the details of history. See Thomas Hodgkin, *Theodoric the Goth* (New York, 1891).

Chapter Four

1. On the collaboration, see Anthony à Wood, *Athenae Oxonienses*, ed. P. Bliss, 4 vols. (London, 1820), vol. 4, col. 209. Because the contributions of the various collaborators cannot now be distinguished, this chapter will discuss the play as if it were entirely the work of Buckingham. On the pre-production history of the play, see *A Key to the Rehearsal* (London: S. Briscoe, 1705), p. xii. More early information about the play is to be found in Montague Summers, *The Playhouse of Pepys* (London, 1935) and Summers' edition of *The Rehearsal* (Stratford-upon-Avon, 1914).

2. Thrall, *A Handbook to Literature*; George H. Nettleton and Arthur E. Case, *British Dramatists from Dryden to Sheridan* (Boston, 1939), pp. 3–5.

3. For a list of the plays which are explicitly parodied in *The Rehearsal*, see pp. 77–80 of the edition by D. E. L. Crane (Durham, 1976). All references to *The Rehearsal* in this chapter are to that edition.

4. Dryden, *Of Dramatic Poesy and Other Critical Essays*, ed. Watson, 1:163–66.

5. Robert F. Willson, Jr., in *"Their Form Confounded": Studies in the Burlesque Play from Udall to Sheridan* (The Hague, 1975), pp. 83–85, suggests that Dryden's key error in the design of this character was his "failure ... to see the impracticability of translating the imaginary realm of heroic poetry into the idiom of the stage." But the fact that Dryden's heroic dramas were popular with contemporary audiences indicates that he made the translation to the satisfaction of his own time.

6. See Richmond P. Bond, *English Burlesque Poetry, 1700–1750* (Cambridge, Mass., 1932); and Peter Lewis, "*The Rehearsal:* A Study of Its Satirical Methods," *Durham University Journal* n.s. 31 (1970):96–113.

7. Charles Gildon, in *The Complete Art of Poetry* (London, 1718), p. 203, reasons as follows: "For either *The Rehearsal*, or the Authors [of heroic drama] were in the wrong; chuse which you will, their promiscuous Applause proves that the Audience must be in the wrong."

8. Crane suggests as approximate analogues *The Conquest of Granada*, part 2 act 3, scene 2; and James Howard's *All Mistaken, or the Mad Couple*, act 5, scene 1.

9. The closest analogue is James Howard's *The English Monsieur*, act 4, scene 1. But see also *The Conquest of Granada*, part 1, act 3, scene 1, and *Tyrannick Love*, act 2, scene 1.

10. See Robert Boyle's *The Black Prince*, act 2, scene 1, and Dryden's *Tyrannick Love*, act 4, scene 1. The Dorset Garden Theatre, which featured elaborate new machinery for "flying" scenery, opened on 9 November 1671, just a month before *The Rehearsal*, so that Buckingham's satire was particularly timely. See Sybil Rosenfeld, *A Short History of Scene Design in Great Britain* (Oxford, 1973), pp. 44–45.

11. Bayes remarks (5. 1. 6) that his scene rivals one in Davenant's *Henry the Eighth* (actually a production of the Shakespeare play in 1663), act 2 scene 4.

12. Horace, *Epistles*, bk. 2, Epistle 3 ["Ars Poetica"], l. 341. This and all quotations from *Ars Poetica* are taken from *Satires and Epistles of Horace*, trans. Smith Palmer Bovie (Chicago: University of Chicago Press, 1959).

13. The danger in the use of the word "classical" is that readers will associate it with certain supposed characteristics (for example, austerity, serenity) of classical literature. As used in this chapter, the term denotes simply the fact that seventeenth-century writers were conscious of working in a tradition which extended back to classical (Greek and Roman) times.

14. Pope, *Essay on Criticism*, l. 73. This and all quotations from Pope are taken from *The Poems of Alexander Pope*, ed. John Butt (New Haven, 1963).

15. Horace, *Ars Poetica*, ll. 268–69.
16. Pope, *Essay on Criticism*, l. 119.
17. Ibid., ll. 163–64.
18. Wilson, *A Rake and His Times*, pp. 199–200.
19. Thomas J. Fujimura, *The Restoration Comedy of Wit* (Princeton, 1952), pp. 65–66.
20. For comment on the meaning of the phrase "blown upon" in the Restoration, see Richard Elias, " 'Bayes' in Buckingham's *The Rehearsal*," *English Language Notes* 15 (1978):178–81.
21. For Rochester's poem, see *The Complete Poems of John Wilmot, Earl of Rochester*, ed. David M. Vieth (New Haven, 1968). For Buckingham's "Epistle to Julian," see any of the editions of his *Miscellaneous Works*, or *Poems on Affairs of State*, 1:387–91.
22. *Poems on Affairs of State*, vol. 3, ed. Howard H. Schless (New Haven, 1968), p. 77. Most biographers of Dryden dismiss the story as obviously inspired by *The Rehearsal*. See, for example, James M. Osborn, *John Dryden: Some Biographical Facts and Problems* (New York, 1940), pp. 160–61.
23. Robert Bell, "John Dryden, 1631–1700," in *The Poems of John Dryden*, 3 vols. (London, 1854), 1:40–41. See also Edmond Malone, "Some Account of the Life and Writings of John Dryden," in *The Critical and Miscellaneous Prose Works of John Dryden*, 3 vols. in 4 (London, 1800), 1:99–100.
24. Spence, *Anecdotes, Observations, and Characters of Books and Men*, p. 63.
25. Thomas Davies, *Dramatic Miscellanies*, 3 vols. (London, 1783), 3:289–90.
26. Dryden, *Of Dramatic Poesy*, 1:116.
27. For example, see Shadwell's *The Medal of John Bayes*, ll. 25–30, in *Poems on Affairs of State*, 3:82; and Rochester's "An Allusion to Horace," ll. 71–76, in *Complete Poems*, p. 124.
28. Lewis, "Satirical Methods," p. 98.
29. Dryden, "A Discourse Concerning the Original and Progress of Satire," in *Of Dramatic Poesy*, 2:77–78.
30. Dryden, *Of Dramatic Poesy*, 1:180; Hume, *Development of the English Drama*, p. 291.
31. George McFadden, "Political Satire in *The Rehearsal*," *Yearbook of English Studies* 4 (1974):120–28.
32. A copy of the 1683 quarto edition of *The Rehearsal* now in the University of Pennsylvania Library bears a marginal annotation in a contemporary hand at this scene reading, "Sr Wm Couentry Sr John Duncomb."

33. See Elizabeth D'Oyley, *James Duke of Monmouth* (London, 1938), pp. 75–77.
34. *The Diary of John Evelyn*, ed. E. S. deBeer, 6 vols. (Oxford, 1955), 4:188.
35. Pepys, *Diary*, 8:79.
36. Evelyn, *Diary*, 3:599.
37. Sheridan Baker, "Buckingham's Permanent Rehearsal," *Michigan Quarterly Review* 12 (1973):169.

Chapter Five

1. *The Complete Works of Thomas Shadwell*, ed. Montague Summers, 5 vols. (London, 1927), 3:193–94.
2. Gunnar Sorelius, "Shadwell Deviating into Sense: *Timon of Athens* and the Duke of Buckingham," *Studia Neophilologia* 36 (1964): 232–44; Alan S. Fisher, "The Significance of Thomas Shadwell," *Studies in Philology* 71 (1974):225–46.
3. Burghclere, *George Villiers*, pp. 315–19, 334.
4. *Complete Works*, 3:19–20, 101–2, 283.
5. They may have collaborated in 1669, with other satirists, in an attack on Edward Howard. See Wilson, *Court Wits*, p. 178.
6. "An Elegy Upon the Death of my Lord Francis Villiers," *The Poems and Letters of Andrew Marvell*, ed. H. M. Margoliouth, 2 vols. (Oxford, 1927), 1:329–332; on the evidence for the attribution of this poem to Marvell, see 1:332–34; Joseph H. Summers, *The Heirs of Donne and Jonson* (New York, 1970), p. 189; and Nicholas Guild, "The Contexts of Marvell's Early 'Royalist' Poems," *Studies in English Literature, 1600–1900* 20 (1980):129.
7. Guild, "Contexts," pp. 125–36; John Dixon Hunt, *Andrew Marvell: His Life and Writings* (Ithaca, 1978), pp. 25, 26; Burghclere, *George Villiers*, pp. 19–20.
8. Marvell, *Poems and Letters*, 2:18, 48, 310–11, 297, 329, 321.
9. *Poems on Affairs of State*, 1:55.
10. Hunt, *Andrew Marvell*, p. 186.
11. *The Rehearsal Transpros'd*, in *The Complete Works of Andrew Marvell, M. P.*, vol. 3, ed. Alexander B. Grosart, 4 vols. (1873; reprint ed., New York, 1966).
12. Dryden's portrait is in *Absalom and Achitophel*, ll. 534–68; for a text, see chapter 1. References to Butler's character "A Duke of Bucks" are to Samuel Butler, *Characters*, ed. Charles W. Daves (Cleveland, 1970), pp. 66–67. Burnet's character is in his *History of My Own Time*, 1:182–83. "On the Prorogation" is in *Poems on Affairs of State*, 1:179–84. The character of Buckingham occupies lines 36–95 of the poem. "A Litany of

the Duke of Buckingham" is in *Poems on Affairs of State*, vol. 2, ed. Elias F. Mengel, Jr. (New Haven, 1965), pp. 192–99. The satire beginning "I sing the praise of a worthy wight" exists in ten manuscript versions, including the following in the British Library: MS Add. 23,722, fols. 3–4^v; MS Harl. 7312, pp. 74–77; and MS Harl. 7315, fols. 46^v–49.

13. For further information on Restoration satirical myth-making, see David M. Vieth's discussion of verse satires on Rochester in *Attribution in Restoration Poetry* (New Haven, 1963), chap. 6, particularly pp. 166–67.

14. Jean Hagstrum, "Verbal and Visual Caricature in the Age of Dryden, Swift, and Pope," in *England in the Restoration and Early Eighteenth Century*, ed. H. T. Swedenberg, Jr. (Berkeley, 1972), p. 192.

15. Emmett L. Avery, "The Stage Popularity of *The Rehearsal*, 1671–1777," *Research Studies, Washington State College* 7 (1939):201–4. See also Hume, *The Development of the English Drama*, p. 23.

16. See Dane Farnsworth Smith, *Plays about the Theatre in England from "The Rehearsal" in 1671 to the Licensing Act of 1737* (London, 1936), pp. 10, 245–46.

17. Sheridan, *The Critic*, in *Eighteenth-Century English Literature*, ed. Geoffrey Tillotson, Paul Fussell, Jr., and Marshall Waingrow (New York, 1969), p. 1378. Future references to *The Critic* are to this edition.

18. *The Complete Works of Henry Fielding*, ed. William Ernest Henley (reprint ed., New York: Barnes and Noble, 1967) 4:197.

19. See Pierre Legouis, "Buckingham et Sheridan: Ce Que le *Critique* Doit à la *Répétition*," *Revue Anglo-américaine* 11 (1934):423–34.

20. See John Loftis, *Sheridan and the Drama of Georgian England* (Cambridge, Mass., 1977), pp. 120–23.

21. V. C. Clinton-Baddeley, *The Burlesque Tradition in the English Theatre after 1660* (1952; reprint ed., London, 1973), pp. 76–77.

22. Review by Brooks Atkinson in the *New York Times*, 27 May 1952, p. 30.

Selected Bibliography

PRIMARY SOURCES

1. Plays

The Chances, A Comedy: As It Was Acted at The Theater Royal. Corrected and Altered by a Person of Honour. London, 1682. Subsequent editions in 1692, 1711, 1735, 1791, 1817, and 1826.

The Country Gentleman: A "Lost" Play and Its Background. Edited by Arthur H. Scouten and Robert D. Hume. Philadelphia: University of Pennsylvania Press, 1976. By Sir Robert Howard and George Villiers, duke of Buckingham. The newly discovered text of the play, with extensive commentary.

The Rehearsal. London, 1672. Four subsequent editions during Buckingham's lifetime, each with additions: 1673, 1675, 1683, 1687. Thirteen further editions through 1777.

The Rehearsal. Edited by Edward Arber. English Reprints, no. 10. London: A. Murray and Son, 1868. Contains a well-illustrated key to the allusions in the burlesque.

The Rehearsal. Edited by Montague Summers. Stratford-upon-Avon: Shakespeare Head Press, 1914. Learned but idiosyncratic and not always reliable.

The Rehearsal. Edited by D. E. L. Crane. Durham, England: Durham University Press, 1976. An authoritative text with a good brief bibliography and thorough notes.

2. Separate Prose Works

The Duke of Buckingham's Speech in a Late Conference. London, 1668.

"The Duke of Buckingham's Speech in the House of Lords, November 16, 1675." In *Two Speeches.* Amsterdam, 1675.

A Letter to Sir Thomas Osborn upon the Reading of a Book called The Present Interest of England. London, 1672.

A Short Discourse of the Reasonableness of Men's Having a Religion, or Worship of God. London, 1685. Two more editions, both 1685.

"A Speech Made by the Duke of Buckingham, the First Day of the Session of the Parliament...15 February 1679." In *State Tracts.* London, 1689.

3. Collected Works

Miscellaneous Works, Written by His Grace, George, Late Duke of Buckingham. London, 1704.

The Second Volume of Miscellaneous Works, Written by George, Late Duke of Buckingham. London, 1705.

The Works of his Grace, George Villiers, Late Duke of Buckingham, 2 vols. London, 1715. Three more editions in 1752, 1754, 1775.

"The Works of George Villiers, Duke of Buckingham." Edited by Thomas Percy, Bishop of Dromore. [1806]. The most authoritative edition of Buckingham's collected works, completed but never published. There is a copy, in 2 volumes, in the British Library.

4. Unpublished Materials

Commonplace book of the duke of Buckingham, in the possession of the earl of Jersey.

SECONDARY SOURCES

1. Books

Beaumont, Francis, and Fletcher, John. *The Dramatic Works in the Beaumont and Fletcher Canon.* Edited by Fredson Bowers. 4 vols. Cambridge: Cambridge University Press, 1966–79. Texts of *The Chances* and *Philaster*, which Buckingham revised.

Burghclere, Winifred. *George Villiers, Second Duke of Buckingham, 1628–1687: A Study in the History of the Restoration.* London: John Murray, 1903. The best-researched source of information on Buckingham's life as a whole.

Burnet, Gilbert. *A History of My Own Time.* Edited by Osmund Airy. 2 vols. Oxford: Clarendon Press, 1897. Contains many references to Buckingham.

Chapman, Hester W. *Great Villiers: A Study of George Villiers, Second Duke of Buckingham, 1628–1687.* London: Secker and Warburg, 1949. Exciting but speculative biography.

Clinton-Baddeley, Victor Clinton. *The Burlesque Tradition in the English Theatre after 1660.* London: Metheun, 1952, reprinted 1973. Good brief account of Buckingham's influence on his successors.

Dryden, John. *The Works of John Dryden.* Edited by H. T. Swedenberg, Jr., Earl Miner, Vinton A. Dearing, and George R. Guffey. 20 vols. Berkeley: University of California Press, 1956–. Texts of several plays burlesqued in *The Rehearsal* and of *Absalom and Achitophel*, which contains the most famous verse portrait of Buckingham.

Hudson, Hoyt. *The Epigram in the English Renaissance.* 1947. Reprint. New York: Octagon, 1966. An excellent critical study of a form in which Buckingham often excelled.

Hume, Robert D. *The Development of The English Drama in the Late Seventeenth Century.* Oxford: Clarendon Press, 1976. The most authoritative discussion of the background and context of Buckingham's dramatic work.

A Key to the Rehearsal. London: Samuel Briscoe, 1705. The earliest attempt to identify the plays burlesqued in Buckingham's greatest work.

Lord, George deForest et al., eds. *Poems on Affairs of State: Augustan Satirical Verse, 1660–1714.* New Haven: Yale University Press, 1963–75. Contains one poem by Buckingham (the "Epistle to Julian") and several which mention him.

Osborn, James Marshall. *John Dryden: Some Biographical Facts and Problems.* New York: Columbia University Press, 1940. Separates myth from fiction regarding references to Dryden in *The Rehearsal.*

Pepys, Samuel. *The Diary of Samuel Pepys.* Edited by Robert Latham and William Matthews. 11 vols. Berkeley: University of California Press, 1970–83. An important source of biographical information about Buckingham.

Smith, Dane Farnsworth. *The Critics in the Audience of the London Theatres from Buckingham to Sheridan: A Study of Neoclassicism in the Playhouse, 1671–1779.* University of New Mexico Publications in Language and Literature, no. 12. Albuquerque: University of New Mexico Press, 1953. Presents *The Rehearsal* as the first important manifestation of the gentleman amateur critic.

──────. *Plays About the Theatre in England from "The Rehearsal" in 1671 to the Licensing Act in 1737.* London: Oxford University Press, 1936. Contains an elaborate analysis of the satiric strategy of *The Rehearsal.*

Sprague, Arthur Colby. *Beaumont and Fletcher on the Restoration Stage.* Cambridge, Mass.: Harvard University Press, 1926. Good discussions of Buckingham's adaptations of *The Chances* and *Philaster.*

Van Lennep, William et al., eds. *The London Stage, 1660–1680.* 5 vols. in 11. Carbondale: Southern Illinois University Press, 1965. An important source of information about production histories.

Willson, Robert F., Jr. *"Their Form Confounded": Studies in the Burlesque Play from Udall to Sheridan.* Paris: Mouton, 1975. Sensible discussion of *The Rehearsal* in relation to its models, predecessors, and successors.

Wilson, John Harold. *The Court Wits of The Restoration: An Introduction.* Princeton: Princeton University Press, 1948. Best available discussion of the context of Buckingham's life and work.

———. *A Rake and His Times: George Villiers Second Duke of Buckingham.* New York: Farrar, Straus, and Young, 1954. Well-researched biography, but limited primarily to the years 1666–74.

2. Articles

Avery, Emmett L. "The Stage Popularity of *The Rehearsal*, 1671–1777." *Research Studies, State College of Washington* 7 (1939):201–4. Valuable information about the production history of the play.

Baker, Sheridan. "Buckingham's Permanent Rehearsal." *Michigan Quarterly Review* 12 (1973):160–71. Excellent critical discussion.

Barrington, Michael. "The Reasonableness of Religion." *Notes and Queries* 195 (1950):432–34, 436. A summary, illustrated with extensive quotations, of the *Short Discourse*, Buckingham's most important nondramatic prose work. Contains no real critical analysis.

Elias, Richard. "'Bayes' in Buckingham's *The Rehearsal*." *English Language Notes* 15 (1978):178–81. The phrase "blown upon" in *The Rehearsal*, act 1, scene 1, line 68, parodies a line in Dryden's *Essay of Dramatic Poesy* (1688). Dryden altered the phrase in later editions.

Emery, John P. "Restoration Dualism of the Court Writers." *Revue des langues vivantes* 32 (1966):238–65. Defends Buckingham and his writings against charges of sexual looseness and atheism.

Fisher, Alan S. "The Significance of Thomas Shadwell," *Studies in Philology* 71 (1974):225–46. Buckingham's alleged influence on Shadwell's political and literary ideas.

Hagstrum, Jean. "Verbal and Visual Caricature in the Age of Dryden, Swift, and Pope." In *England in the Restoration and Early Eighteenth Century*, edited by H. T. Swedenberg, Jr. Berkeley: University of California Press, 1972. Discusses Dryden's caricature of Buckingham as "Zimri."

Jason, Phillip K. "A Twentieth-Century Response to *The Critic*." *Theatre Survey* 15 (1974):51–58. Includes discussion of Buckingham's influence on Sheridan.

Legouis, Pierre. "Buckingham et Sheridan: ce que le *Critique* doit à la *Répétition*." *Revue anglo-américaine* 11 (1934):423–34. The influence of *The Rehearsal* on *The Critic*.

Lewis, Peter. "*The Rehearsal*: A Study of Its Satirical Methods." *Durham University Journal*, n.s. 31 (1970):96–113. Detailed, somewhat elementary, analysis.

Macey, Samuel L. "Fielding's *Tom Thumb* as the Heir to Buckingham's *Rehearsal*." *Texas Studies in Literature and Language* 10 (1968):405–14. *Tom Thumb* in the *Rehearsal* tradition.

McFadden, George. "Political Satire in *The Rehearsal*." *Yearbook of*

English Studies 4 (1974):120–28. Well-researched, but more suggestive than conclusive.
Orwen, William R. "Marvell and Buckingham." *Notes and Queries* 196 (1951):10–11. Possible influence of Marvel's *Horatian Ode* on Buckingham's elegy for Fairfax.
Roebuck, Graham. "A 'New' Portrait by Clarendon." *Notes and Queries* 20 (1973):168–70. Argues (unconvincingly) that an untitled prose character in Clarendon's manuscripts is of Buckingham.
Smith, John Harrington. "Dryden and Buckingham: The Beginnings of the Feud." *Modern Language Notes* 69 (1954):242–45. Dates the theatrical rivalry from 1667, when *The Chances* and Dryden's *Secret Love* shared popularity.
Sorelius, Gunnar. "Shadwell Deviating Into Sense: Timon of Athens and the Duke of Buckingham." *Studia Neophilologica* 36 (1964):232–44. Finds references to Buckingham in Shadwell's revision of *Timon of Athens*.

3. Dissertations

Mizener, Arthur. "George Villiers Second Duke of Buckingham: His Life and a Canon of His Works." Ph.D. dissertation, Princeton University, 1934. Outdated on Buckingham's life, but still valuable as a discussion of his canon.

Index

Addison, 125
Althaea, 24
Amboyna, Massacre of, 45
Apollo, 26
Aristotle, 87
Arlington, Henry Bennet, earl of, 7, 8, 11–14, 20, 38–39, 107–109, 124, 127
Arran, Richard Butler, earl of, 19–20
Artemis, 26
Atropos, 24, 26
Aurora, 34–35

Baker, Sheridan, 109
Barillon, Paul, ambassador of France, 4, 13
Bayes, 14
Beaumont, Francis, 52; *Philaster: or Love Lies a-Bleeding*, 69–73, 124. See also Fletcher, John
Blank verse, 71-72, 76, 78–79, 123
Blood, Colonel Thomas, 115
Bologna, 52, 59
Brecht, Berthold: *Threepenny Opera*, 124
Brentford, 82
Bridgewater, 74
Burlesque poetry, 30
Burlesque drama, 81–87, 109
Burnet, Gilbert, bishop, 4, 8, 20, 116–18
Butler, Charlotte, 119
Butler, Samuel, 81, 116; "A Duke of Bucks," 117–18

Cabal ministry, 11–12, 13, 14, 20, 107, 114
Cambridge University, 2–3, 13, 113, 124
Cartwright, William, 115
Castle Helmsley, 19
Catherine of Braganza, queen of England, 8, 17
Catholicism, 2, 12–13, 17, 44, 74
Catullus, 22
Cervantes, Miguel de: *La Senora Cornelia*, 52
Chain of Being, 28, 129n11
Charles I, king of England, 1, 4, 21, 44
Charles II, king of England, 2, 4, 6, 7, 8, 9, 10, 11–13, 16, 17, 19, 20, 38, 62–64, 107, 114
Chertsey, 2
Chesterfield, Philip Stanhope, earl of, 5
Churchill, John (later first duke of Marlborough), 74
Cibber, Colley, 120
Cibber, Theophilus, 120
Cincinnatus, 29
Civil Wars, 3–4, 29, 44
Clarendon, Edward Hyde, earl of, 4, 5, 7, 8–9, 20, 114, 124, 128n10
Clifford, Martin, 3, 6, 45, 81, 112
Clifford, Thomas, baron, 11, 12, 13
Clive, Catherine, 120
Commonplace Book, 21
Country Party (Whigs), 16–19, 112
Court Wits, 51, 112

Index

"Coventry, earl of" (illegitimate son of second duke of Buckingham), 11, 26
Coventry, Sir William, 9, 62–64, 65, 107–108
Cowley, Abraham, 2, 6, 112, 113; *The Mistress*, 2; *Naufragium Joculare*, 113; *Davideis*, 2
Cromwell, Oliver, lord protector, 5–6, 30, 44, 112–13

Dance, James, 120
D'Avenant, Sir William, 103; *The Play-house to Be Let*, 120
Davies, Sir John, 22
Davies, Thomas: *Dramatic Miscellanies*, 103
Decorum as critical principle, 96
Denham, Sir John, 6
Donne, John, 2; "The Relic," 23; "The Ecstasy," 36–37, 125
Dorchester, Henry Pierrepont, marquis of, 114
Dorset Garden Theatre, 133n10
Dover, Treaty of, *12–13*, 15, 41
Dryden, John, 18, 23–26, 61, 81, 102–107, 124–25; *Absalom and Achitophel*, 18, *23–26*, 116–19; *The Conquest of Granada*, 82–84, 93, 106, 133n9; "Defense of an Essay of Dramatic Poesy," 105; *Defense of the Epilogue*, 70, 106; *Discourse Concerning the Original and Progress of Satire*, 106, 110; *Marriage a la Mode*, 64; *The Medal*, 103; *Tyrannick Love*, 85–86, 91
Duncomb, Sir John, 62, 65, 107
Dutch Wars (1665–67), 8; (1673–74), 13, 15, *41–44*
Dutton, William, 113

East India Companies, 43–44
Edward IV, king of England, 5
Elizabeth I, queen of England, 21, 66
Entrapment, rhetorical, 46–50
Epigram, 21–29
Estcourt, Richard, 120
Etherege, Sir George: *The Man of Mode*, 64
Evelyn, John, 108–109
Exclusion Crisis, 4, 17–19, 46

Fairfax, Anne, baroness, 29
Fairfax, Brian, 5
Fairfax, Thomas, baron, 5–6, 11, *29–32*, 37, 112–13, 115, 124
Fawkes, Guy, 44
Felton, John, 2
Feversham, Louis de Duras, earl of, 73–76
Fielding, Henry: *The Author's Farce*, 120, 122; *Pasquin*, 121, 122; *The Tragedy of Tragedies, or the Life and Death of Tom Thumb the Great*, 122
Finch, Heneage (later earl of Nottingham), 27, 128n10
Fisher, Alan S., 111–12
Fletcher, John, 9, 65; *The Chances*, 53–54, 59, 61–62, 70, 106; *Philaster: or, Love Lies a-Bleeding*, 69–73, 124
Folger Shakespeare Library, 62
Foote, Samuel, 120

Garrick, David, 119, 120
"Gay couple" tradition in comedy, 66
Gay, John: *The Beggar's Opera*, 122, 123, 124; *The What d'Ye Call It*, 122
Godfrey, Sir Edmund Berry, 17

Grammont, Philippe, comte de, 3, 76, 125
Grey, Ford, baron, 74
Gunpowder Plot, 44
Gwynne, Nell, 8, 119

Hagstrum, Jean, 119
Harrington, Sir John, 22
Hart, Charles, 119
Henrietta Maria, queen of England, 2
Henry VIII, king of England, 12
Heroic drama, 81, 123
Herrick, Robert, 28
Hesperus, 34–35
Heydon, John, 8
Holmes, Sir Robert, 10
Homer: *Iliad*, 83
Horace, 87, 88, 96
House of Commons, 2, 16, 74
House of Lords, 9, 15–16, 17, 45
Howard, Bernard, 10
Howard, Sir Robert, 9, 52, 64–65, 67–69, 97, 103
Hull, 113–14
Hume, Robert D., 62, 64, 106
Hyperbole, 22–23

Imagination ("Fancy"), 92, 94, 98
Iphigenia, 45
"I sing the praise of a worthy wight," 116

James I, king of England, 1
James II, king of England, 2, 19, 46, 73, 130n22; as duke of York, 8, 12, 17, 62, 64, 107–108, 112
Jenkins, William, 10
Jonson, Ben, 22
Judgment, 23, 36, 48

Killigrew, Harry, 10
Killigrew, Thomas, 63
Kynaston, Edward, 117, 131n7

Lacy, John, 104, 115, 120
Landor, William Savage, 28
Latona, 26
Laud, William, archbishop of Canterbury, 2
Lauderdale, John Maitland, earl and duke of, 11
Lessing, Gotthold Ephraim, 22
Licensing Act (1737), 121
"A Litany of the Duke of Buckingham," 116
Litchfield Close, battle of, 3
Lockier, Dean Francis, 3, 104, 106
London, 66, 82, 90; Treaty of, 13
Louis XIV, king of France, 1, 7, 12–14, 15, 44, 74
"Love duels," 66
Lovelace, Richard, 21
Lucretius: *De Rerum Natura*, 45

McFadden, George, 107
Martial, 21
Marvell, Andrew, 29, 112–16, 129n15; *Horatian Ode upon Cromwell's Return from Ireland*, 113, 129n15; *The Rehearsal Transpros'd*, 115
Mary Tudor, queen of England, 12, 44, 46
Meleager, 24, 26
Milton, John, 115
Molière, *Impromptu de Versailles*, 120
Monck, George, 6
Monmouth, James Scott, duke of, 14, 17, 74; Monmouth's Rebellion, 51, 74, 108
Moses, 18, 25

Nature, 87–89, 92
Newcastle, Henry Cavendish, (second) duke of, 39–40

Newcastle, William Cavendish, first duke of, 40
Nicole, Pierre, *Essay on True and Apparent Beauty*, 22–23
Nun Appleton House, 11, 29, 113

Oldfield, Anne, 119
"On the Prorogation," 116
Order of the Garter, 39–40
Osborne, Thomas, earl of Danby, 17, 20, 39–41
Ossory, Thomas Butler, earl of, 14

Paradox, 22
Paris, 4, 10
Parker, Samuel, 115
Parliament, 4–6, 12, 14, 15–17, 30, 44
Parody, 82–86, 91, 93
Pepys, Samuel, 10, 11, 63, 108, 118
Petition of Right, 2
Phinehas, 25
Plague of 1665, 25
Plantagenet, house of, 5
Pindaric Ode, 29–32
Pope, Alexander: *Essay on Criticism*, 88–89, 125
"Popish Plot," 17
Portsmouth, Louise de Querouale, duchess of, 8
Present Interest of England Stated, The, 41–42
Prior, Matthew, 28
Privy Council, 9, 11, 62–63, 108
Protestantism, 44

Raleigh, Sir Walter, 21
Ram Alley, 27
Reeve, Anne, 106
Restoration of English monarchy, 5–6, 29, 114
Rich, Henry, earl of Holland, 4
Richmond, Mary Villiers Stuart Howard, duchess of (sister of second duke of Buckingham), 8, 117
Rochester, John Wilmot, earl of, 51, 100, 124
Rome, 3
Royal Society, 6
Rubens, 5
Rupert, Prince, 3
Rules of criticism, 88–89, 94–95
Rye House Plot, 46

Sackville, Charles, earl of Dorset, 6, 105
St. George, 40
Sandwich, Edward Montague, earl of, 7, 114
Satire, 24; personal, 37–40, 102–109, 116–19; political, 73, 107–109, 123
Saville, Henry, 63
Scotland, 4, 30
Scouten, Arthur H., 62, 64
Scroop, Sir Carr, 38–39
Sedgmoor, Battle of, 74
Sedley, Sir Charles, 6, 63, 131n7
Shadwell, Thomas, 111–12; *The Medal of John Bayes*, 103; *Timon of Athens*, 111, 112
Shaftesbury, Anthony Ashley Cooper, earl of, 11, 14, 17–18, 72, 103
Shakespeare, William: *Hamlet*, 56; *A Midsummer Night's Dream*, 120; *Othello*, 70–71, 123
Sheridan, Richard Brinsley: *The Critic*, 120–23
Shrewsbury, Anna-Maria, countess of, 9–11, 15–16, 18, 25, 26, 37, 114, 116–17
Shrewsbury, Charles Talbot, twelfth earl of, 15
Shrewsbury, Francis Talbot, eleventh earl of, 10–11, 63, 117

Sidney, Sir Philip, 21
Smith, Dane Farnsworth, 121
Soliloquy, 59–60
Spence, Joseph, 104
Spenser, Edmund: *Epithalamium*, 35
Sprague, Arthur Colby, 61
Sprat, Thomas, 6, 81, 112
Standing army, 73
Stapylton, Robert: *The Slighted Maid*, 91
Stop of the Exchequer, 14–15
Stoppard, Tom: *Rosencrantz and Guildenstern Are Dead*, 55–56
Stuart, Frances, 7
Suckling, Sir John, 21
Suffolk, earl of, 2
Surbiton Common, battle of, 4
Sweden, 41
Swift, Jonathan, 46, 125; *A Tale of a Tub*, 125

Talbot, Sir John, 10
Tasso, Torquato: *Jerusalem Delivered*, 83
Test Act, 15, 44, 114
Theatre Royal, 63
Tithonus, 34–35
Titian, 5
Toleration, religious, 7, 16–17, 44–51, 112
Tower of London, 6, 9, 17, 39, 63–64, 112, 114
Triple Alliance, 41
Turenne, Marshal, 74

Unity, 89, 93–94, 96

Venus, 35
Vernell, Peter, 108
Villiers, Francis, 2–4, 112–13
Villiers, George, first duke of Buckingham, 1, 5, 7

Villiers, George, second duke of Buckingham, attacks Sir William Coventry in *The Country Gentleman*, 9, 62–64; attends Cambridge University, 2–3, 113; attempts to lead uprisings against Cromwell, 4; becomes father of illegitimate son, 11, 114; birth, 2; charged with adultery in House of Lords, 15–16; coaches Lacy in part of Bayes, 104; conducts affair with countess of Shrewsbury, 9–11; confined to Tower of London, 6, 17, 112; duels with earl of Shrewsbury, 9–11, 63; engages in espionage for Charles II, 5, 115; impeached by House of Commons, 16; leads Country Party during Exclusion Crisis, 17–19; makes Grand Tour, 3; marries Mary Fairfax, 5; maneuvers against earl of Clarendon, 7–9; member of Cabal ministry, 11–16; negotiates sham Treaty of Dover, 13; reputation as irreligious, 47; satirized in *Absalom and Achitophel*, 18–19, 23–26, 116–19; thwarts attempted assassination, 27, 128n9; writes *The Rehearsal*, 14

WORKS: POETRY
"Advice to a Painter to Draw my Lord Arlington, Grand Minister of State," 39
"Breasts," 26
"Earth, air, and water we depopulate," 28
"Epitaph on Thomas, third Lord Fairfax," 29–32, 36, 40, 124, 129n15
"Epithalamium," 32, 34–35, 40
"Familiar Epistle to Mr. Julian,

Index

Secretary to the Muses," 38–39, 40, 100
"Love," 32–33
"Love's flame kept in," 27–28
"Nature ne'er leaps," 28
"On the Late Lord Chancellor," 27, 29, 38
"Some eyes so bright," 22
"The Lost Mistress," 32, 33–34
"To Dryden," 23–26, 29, 35, 40
"To his Mistress," 32, 35–37, 40
"What strange injustice in my fate," 22
"Upon the Installment," 39–40

WORKS: DRAMA
Battle of Sedgmoor Rehearsed at Whitehall: A Farce, The, 73–76, 80
Chances, The, 9, 52–61, 64–65, 80, 106, 119, 124
Country Gentleman, The, 9, 62–69, 73, 80, 97, 102, 107
Rehearsal, The, 3, 14, 20, 52, 65, 73, 79, 81–110, 119–25
Restauration: or, Right Will Take Place, The, 69–73, 80, 124
Untitled Blank Verse Heroic Fragment, 76–80

WORKS: PROSE
"Letter to Martin Clifford," 45–46

Letter to Sir Thomas Osborn, A, 15, 41–44
Short Discourse upon the Reasonableness of Men's Having a Religion, or Worship of God, A, 19, 44–50

Villiers, Kathryn Manners, duchess of Buckingham (mother of second duke), 2
Villiers, Mary Fairfax, duchess of Buckingham (wife of second duke), 5, 10, 11, 29, 113–14, 118

Waller, Edmund, 6
Wallingford House, 6, 11
Walters, Lucy, 17
Wase, Christopher: "Divination," 114
Weill, Kurt: *Threepenny Opera*, 124
Wildman, Major John, 10, 114
Wilson, John Harold, 90
Windsor Castle, 39
Wit, 2–3, 23, 28, 36, 57, 89, 105
Witchcraft, 23–26, 40
Worcester, battle of, 4
Wren, Christopher, 6
Wyatt, Sir Thomas, 21, 22

York House, 13

Zeus, 26

A